400 Ways to Save A Fortune

Other Titles by Annie Jean Brewer

Annie has written a number of fiction and nonfiction titles. Free samples and a variety of purchase links to all her works are available at http://annienygma.com/book-list/. Enjoy!

The Shoestring Girl: How I Live on Practically Nothing and You Can Too
How to Start Out or Over on a Shoestring
How I Designed My Life Using the Law of Attraction and You Can Too
Minimize to Maximize: Minimize Your Stuff to Maximize Your Life
Stay At Home, Mom - Even if You're Single!
Talk Cheap: Your Guide to Free and Cheap Phone Service
How to Survive the Death of Windows XP
How to Watch Stuff Online For Free
How to Write Ebooks for a Living
The Minimalist Cleaning Method
How to Write and Sell an Ebook
Where to Work Online
Professional Help: How to Prevent and Fix Malware, Viruses, Spyware and Other Baddies
Be Happy Now
How to Be Happy
How to Stop a Puppy From Chewing
Four Years as a Writer

Fiction Titles

163 Nights
The Bean Pot and Other Tales
What About Bob?

400 Ways To Save A Fortune

Annie Jean Brewer

First published in ebook format worldwide in 2011.

By Annie Jean Brewer

Annienygma.com

2014 PRINT EDITION

Copyright 2014 by Annie Jean Brewer

PUBLISHED BY:

Annie Jean Brewer on CreateSpace

All rights reserved. No part of this publication may be reproduced, stored in a retrieval system or transmitted by any means, electronic, mechanical, photocopying or otherwise without written permission from the author.

In Loving Memory of

Theo Lewis

May 1, 1925 - December 15, 2013

You are missed.

Table of Contents

Introduction to the 2014 Print Edition..........9

Introduction to the 2011 ebook edition......16

Auto..20

Cleaning..29

Clothing 41

Computers..48

Entertainment...58

Finance 65

Food 74

Gardening...88

General Household.....................................91

Housing 109

Kids 115

Personal Care..119

Pets 138

Shopping 147

Travel 156

Utilities..158

Conclusion 176
Appendix 178
About the Author 253

Introduction to the 2014 Print Edition

It has been several years since I first assembled this collection of tips. Back in those days I was working at what would be my last public job as I penned books during my down time. Thanks to extreme frugality and hard work I managed to retire just a few months after this book was originally published - at the incredible age of 41.

If it were not for many of the tips in this book, my daughter would be spending the last few years of her childhood as a latch key kid, left on her own while I worked to provide for our needs. Instead I have been able to support us with my book royalties for several years now — but I wouldn't have been able to make it happen without frugality.

I used the tips in this book to make the leap to retirement. I had to, because when I quit my day job our income went from about $1,500 a month to $500 a month (my book royalty income at the time). My daughter and I wanted this so much though it wasn't a sacrifice, it was the achievement of a dream.

I make a bit more than $500 a month these days but out of habit I still keep our monthly expenses capped at that $500 limit. It keeps me humble and reminds me of my early days as a single mom when I had to support three kids on even less than that.

My daughter and I live in a small, one-bedroom house, shop for clothing at thrift shops and yard sales, use plastic on the windows in the winter and use a MagicJack as our primary phone service. I sold my van and now walk or use public transportation (I live in a small town with buses available by appointment) when we need to go somewhere. Instead of owning a television we watch shows and stuff online at sites like Netflix nowadays but at first we used many of the free advertising-based sites available on the Internet.

We buy the cheapest bathroom tissue around these days because we don't own a dryer and lack the available space to dry Family Cloths like we did in the past. We even use vinegar as our primary cleaning solution and microfiber cloths for keeping our home clean.

Some things have changed since I originally wrote this book, however. For us, it is now cheaper to purchase a $3 container of laundry detergent instead of making it from scratch. A container lasts us for almost a year. Also, since it is so hard to locate the soap to make dishwashing liquid in my area (and it costs a fortune to order it online) I now spend $1 at the local store for a bottle that lasts us for so long that I can't remember when I bought it last.

I've also learned about some new ways to save money since I wrote this book originally. As a result I've updated this print edition to include over 100 new tips as well as rephrased some of the original ones to make them more readable.

I'm also going to include an appendix in this edition that contains any of my articles that I referenced in the ebook version for your convenience. In addition, any articles I have since published that may help you to save money will be included as well.

Frugality is far from dead, even in this consumerist society. With so many of us dependent upon a single source of income — an income based upon the fickle whims of greedy employers and their lack of loyalty to the ones who actually do the work — we all need to know how to stretch our money as far as it can go in the event that the unthinkable happens.

Even better, there is now another use for extreme frugality. Properly applied, you can actually use the tips in this book to not only save money but to break free from the rat race and pursue your dreams. By lowering your expenses as much as possible you can free some time from working to develop an alternate income source that can allow you to break free from your public job if you so desire. Once you break free you will be able to work on your new career as much as you like, and build up your income to the point where frugality is no longer a necessity, as I did after leaving the public workforce.

Whatever your reasons for embracing frugality, I wish you the absolute best. It is my hope that these tips enable you to achieve *your* goals, as they have done mine.

Sincerely,

Annie Jean Brewer
July, 2014

Disclaimer

The tips in this book are provided for educational purposes only. The author is not responsible for any loss, real or implied, that may occur as a result of trying the tips in this book. Please consult the appropriate professional for advice before undertaking any of the drastic money saving measures found in this book.

Introduction to the 2011 ebook edition

"He that can live sparingly need not be rich."

- Benjamin Franklin

There are tons of frugal living books and websites available. Type the phrase *"how to save money"* into a search engine and you will retrieve tons and tons of tips. Search on one of the ebook websites and you will find a mountain of titles.

Being a hard-core frugalista I've been pouring over these tips and tricks for years. If a frugality ebook sounds like it may provide some more relevant tips I devour it.

One day I bought an ebook only to discover that it contained an introduction, a brief list of generic tips and no ending. The tips just stopped. I was more than a little irritated even though it didn't cost that much. While I probably would have been a bit more satisfied if the book had contained at least a conclusion it demonstrated with clarity why frugality books catch so much crap: some writers are too frugal with their information!

On that day this book was born. The number 400 just came to me though I had no clue if I could even come up with 400 different ways a user could save money. Regardless, I knew it had to be written so I brainstormed, researched and picked the brains of everyone I knew. Even my 12-

year old Katie contributed some tips to this book, to give you an idea of how determined I was.

I have tried to come up with a little bit for everyone and offer alternatives where available. There are tips within that can save thousands of dollars alongside others that may save a few pennies or an extra trip to the store. I have worked hard to ensure that no tip is duplicated though some of these tips may compliment others or offer a different frugal solution.

These tips are separated into general categories to make it easier to search for related subject matter but otherwise they are not placed in any particular order. Choose what tips you like and leave the rest for later.

When you are finished with this book please leave an honest review on the website where you purchased it to help others determine if this book will help them to save money as well. Thank you.

Sincerely,

Annie Jean Brewer

Auto

1. Pay cash for your car. This will save you hundreds (if not thousands) of dollars in interest payments.

2. Pay extra on your car payment every month. This will pay down your principle much faster and save money on interest payments.

3. Keep the car you have. It is cheaper to repair and maintain a vehicle you already own than it is to purchase a new one.

4. If your vehicle is older drop the full-coverage insurance and instead opt for the state-minimum liability. After your car reaches a certain age you will come out ahead by saving the difference because insurance companies are notorious for NOT paying you what your older car is worth.

5. Do you really need a car? You can save a fortune by walking, biking, using public transportation or riding with a friend instead of owning a car yourself.

6. If you own several vehicles eliminate the ones you don't drive regularly. This will save you in taxes, insurance, maintenance and other fees.

7. Cars are a financial liability, not an asset. They cost you money every single month you own them in taxes and insurance alone even if you never drive them. Their only purpose is to get you from Point A to Point B. With this

in mind, buy the cheapest car that will reliably do what you need.

8. Never buy a new car. Cars depreciate an incredible amount as soon as you drive them off the lot. Don't pay for the privilege. Older cars hold their value *much* better.

9. When shopping for a used car have the vehicle inspected before purchase. This can save you a fortune by preventing the purchase of a defective vehicle.

10. Walk or ride a bike for short trips instead of using a car. This will save gas as well as wear and tear on your vehicle.

11. If you go long stretches without driving your vehicle, start it at least once a month and allow it to idle for several minutes. This keeps the fluids circulating in the vehicle and helps to keep the battery charged. My mechanic was always nagging me about this

because I never remembered to do it and had to get my van jump started when the battery ran low.

12. Disconnect your battery cables if you are going to allow your vehicle to sit for longer than a month. Modern vehicles drain the battery even when you aren't using them and they *will* drain your battery dry - or at the least decrease your battery's lifespan.

13. Maintain proper tire pressure for optimum fuel economy. Check at least once a month.

14. Check the air pressure in your spare tire regularly and verify that you have a jack and tire changing tools on hand and in working order. This can save you a long wait and an expensive service call in the event of a flat tire.

15. Check your air filter and change it regularly. A clogged air filter will decrease your fuel economy.

16. Check the fluid levels regularly even in a new car. I always did this when I filled up the fuel tank. Even newer vehicles can get a leak—catching this early will mean the difference between a simple repair and an expensive disaster.

17. Shop around for auto insurance both near and far whenever your premium becomes due. Insurance companies will charge as much as they think they can get out of you and some that are considered cheap are much more expensive than others. I went from paying $150 a month for liability car insurance to less than $50 a month by just shopping around whenever my premiums came due.

18. Drive your car as little as possible to minimize fuel cost and wear on the machine.

19. If you have several stops in one area, park the car in a central spot and walk to all of the places.

20. Do not idle your car any more than you have to; idling reduces your gas mileage to 0.

21. Do not exceed the speed limit. You will save a fortune by avoiding speeding ticket fines.

22. Watch where you park and avoid parking in a no-parking zone. Also ensure that you feed the meters to avoid expensive parking tickets. Avoid parking in a metered spot to save even more.

23. Increase your car insurance deductible to lower your premiums.

24. Drop full-coverage insurance in favor of liability if you own an older car. Stash the premium difference in the bank to save up for another vehicle just

in case your car is totaled in an accident and it is ruled to be your fault.

25. Get an estimate before you let a repair shop even TOUCH your car and make them stick to it. Unless you know the business in question, skipping this part is like writing the word "SUCKER" on your forehead.

26. Know about how much your auto repairs should cost. If you don't you could end up spending $$$$ for a $$ job.

27. Don't replace your vehicle if the motor or transmission fails. If you replace that failed part with a rebuilt engine or transmission you will have the equivalent of a new one (complete with warranty) for a *lot* less than a brand new vehicle would cost.

28. Rotate your tires regularly to make them last longer.

29. If you don't drive much, don't spend the extra money on high-end tires. They will dry-rot before they wear out. This tip comes from a tire salesman, who told me that even the inexpensive tires will dry rot before they wear out if you don't drive your vehicle a lot. Discuss your needs with a professional to get the best tire for your money.

30. Take a general auto maintenance class if available. You will learn tips and tricks to make your car last longer.

31. Keep your car clean both inside and outside. This will keep the interior in good shape and help the paint job to last longer.

32. Avoid parking your car under a tree. The sap from some trees can literally eat the paint from your vehicle. Also, during a storm tree limbs can break off and damage your expensive investment.

33. Invest in a locking gas cap to deter thieves. Regardless of where you live this is a must to protect your expensive fuel investment — especially with today's fuel prices.

34. Keep your car doors locked and any items stashed within out of plain view. You will be surprised at how sticky the neighbor's fingers are! For instance, I used to keep batteries in my car for an MP3 player. I thought my daughter was using them for hers because every time I went to get a battery they were all gone. One day I happened to look outside and discovered the neighbor's kid helping himself to *my* batteries to power *his* video game. Lesson learned.

Cleaning

35. Remove candle wax from the bottom of holders, saucers, plates, etc., by placing them in the freezer. The wax will shrink and come right out without an expensive remover.

36. Avoid taking your laundry to the dry cleaners. Use a cup of ammonia and no soap and wash wool blankets in the washer. You can also do this if you wash them by hand because ammonia does not require rinsing.

37. If you run out of laundry detergent use a cup of ammonia in your wash instead.

38. Singles and small families can save on laundry bills by washing laundry by hand instead of using a Laundromat. This is the norm in many countries even today.

39. Hang your freshly-washed laundry on a clothesline or a drying rack to avoid the expense of owning a dryer or drying your clothes at the laundromat.

40. Hanging whites outside in the sunshine will help to keep them white.

41. Spritz white laundry with lemon juice and hang them outside to help whiten stained whites naturally.

42. Use ammonia instead of bleach to whiten whites occasionally. This will remove the dirt that bleach and traditional detergents leave behind.

43. Make your own liquid laundry detergent[1]. Use 1/2 bar of grated Fels Naptha soap, 1 cup each of Washing Soda and borax. Heat these ingredients in a heavy pan filled with water until the Fels Naptha melts. Add a couple of inches of warm water to a five-gallon bucket then add the melted soap mixture into the bucket and fill to the halfway mark with water. Stir well and leave overnight to cure. The next day stir and mix in enough water to fill the bucket to the top. Dilute this mixture half and half when refilling your liquid laundry detergent containers. Makes 10 gallons. Use 1/2 cup on lightly soiled loads, 3/4 cup on heavy soil.

44. Make your own dishwashing liquid[2]. Grate 1/2 bar of Zote or Octagon soap. Add to a heavy pan with 1 quart of water. Heat over medium heat until the

---

[1] See appendix for details.

[2] See appendix for details.

soap is completely melted. Pour into a 1.5 gallon container and add 3 more quarts of warm water. Shake well. Makes 1 gallon of dishwashing liquid.

45. Use Zote or Octagon soap to wash your dishes instead of buying dishwashing liquid. Place the bar in the sink and fill with water. Lather your cloth or sponge with the bar or soap and wash your dishes. Rinse well and dry.

46. Wash dishes by hand instead of using a dishwasher to save electricity, water and money. Fill two dishpans with warm water. Add dishwashing liquid to one and a tablespoon of vinegar to the other. Wash in the soapy water and rinse in the vinegar water. Dry well. *Note*: You don't have to add vinegar to the rinse water but it helps to eliminate spots.

47. Wash and dry windows using microfiber cloths. Scrub the dirty

window with a wet microfiber cloth (no cleaner needed) and use another microfiber cloth to dry. This leaves a streak-free shine using no chemicals.

48. Most items can be cleaned with warm water and a microfiber cloth so save your cleaning solutions and money.

49. A damp microfiber cloth will both clean and remove germs from the surfaces in your home with no chemical residue. Toss the cloth in the wash to avoid transferring them to other areas when you are done.

50. When you are cleaning with a microfiber cloth, fold and re-fold the cloth to expose new, clean surfaces as you go along to both extend the amount you can clean while avoiding cross-contamination[3].

---

[3] Here is a video that explains the process **https://www.youtube.com/watch?v=MGwVhi9LyVo**

51. Use a magic eraser and water to clean stubborn dirt. These are excellent for removing marks from paint, cleaning tub rings and other ground-in dirt. No chemicals needed.

52. Ammonia and water makes an easy no-rinse cleaner. Add 1 cup of ammonia to a gallon of water.

53. Opening the windows on occasion will help to air out unpleasant odors and freshen rooms and homes.

54. In times past mattresses were placed outside in the sunshine (on clean sheets) to air out and freshen. They were flipped at midday and brought in before the dew settled. Try this tip to avoid replacing smelly mattresses. I spritz mine with vinegar when I do this because vinegar helps remove odors as well.

55. Pillows can be hung outside on clotheslines to freshen. Shake them well when bringing them in to fluff them.

56. Occasionally treat your leather items to a coat of leather polish. This will greatly increase their life span. Even a light coat of mineral oil will help increase their life span if polish is not available.

57. Vinegar and water is an excellent no-rinse window cleaner; use 1 cup of vinegar per gallon of water. My father swore by this recipe for cleaning windows and refused to use anything else.

58. Mop carpets instead of spending money on a carpet shampooer. Vacuum thoroughly and mop with a mixture of 1 cup ammonia (some prefer vinegar) per gallon of warm water. Change water as needed. Allow to dry and then vacuum again to remove the extra stubborn dirt that the mopping

dislodged but didn't remove. In my opinion this gets carpets cleaner and fresher than an expensive shampooer. Test your carpet in an inconspicuous area before mopping the whole carpet just in case.

59. Store steel wool pads in the freezer between uses. This prevents them from rusting.

60. If you own a washing machine, wash your clothes in cold water. It saves the money needed to heat that water and your clothes will be just as clean.

61. Wear your clothing more than once before you wash it. Hang it up and allow to air out between wearings to get several uses out of it before you have to wash.

62. Reuse bath towels several times before you launder them. It sounds gross but you are drying your clean body with a

clean towel. It isn't as dirty as you think.

63. Don't have a mountain of damp towels stuffed on your towel rack. They will sour and force you to wash them sooner. One is sufficient.

64. Have separate towels for hands and body. The hand towel will get dirtier much faster than the one you use for your body.

65. Turn your hand towel around at least once a day. This allows the front side to dry before being used again because most people only grab the front layer when they dry their hands.

66. Keep your sponges clean and fresh: Rinse well after use and microwave for 30 seconds to kill any remaining germs within.

67. One half cup of white vinegar added to the rinse cycle makes a frugal and effective fabric softener.

68. Clean the coils behind your refrigerator and freezer occasionally. Dust will reduce their efficiency and increase their energy usage.

69. Inspect the fans on refrigerators and freezers occasionally. Once I thought I would need a service call because my freezer was not keeping things cold. I pulled it out from the wall to see what was wrong and discovered that a mouse had unsuccessfully tried to race the fan blades. I removed the remains and the freezer worked perfectly after that. Gross but true.

70. A small bowl of vinegar will help to dispel odors in the home.

71. Make a sachet of coffee grounds (unused is best) and store in your

refrigerator to dispel odors instead of baking soda.

72. If your refrigerator or freezer smells really nasty, clean well with a vinegar and water solution then place a small bowl of fresh coffee grounds inside and close it up (leaving the appliance running helps here). Stir the grounds every day and replace them with fresh once a week. I once saved a chest freezer that had been filled with meat during an extended power outage using this trick. When I started working on it the stench was so bad it made you want to gag but this method eliminated the odors and the freezer is still in use today.

73. Clean out the lint that builds up in your dryer vent and in your dryer occasionally. This lint reduces the efficiency of your dryer and can also cause a fire.

74. You don't need to buy expensive cleaners to clean your commode. Instead, pour a splash of bleach, ammonia or dishwashing liquid (I've even used shampoo in a pinch) into your commode. Scrub well and flush to clean on the cheap. Only use one of these cleaners at a time - they don't play well together!

75. Leave shoes outside of the house or just inside the front door when entering. This will keep a large amount of dirt outside and therefore save money in cleaning supplies.

Clothing

76. Only keep enough clothing to last you until laundry day (about a week or so). If your wardrobe is bigger than that some items will be lost in your closet and forgotten.

77. Socks and underwear can be washed whenever you bathe and easily hung up to dry for the next use.

78. Cloth purses can be tossed in a washer instead of dry-cleaned or washed separately.

79. Keep a single outfit to wear for when you are doing something that may stain your clothing (like painting). Even if that outfit gets a stain or two who cares? Keep using it until it falls apart and then designate another work outfit to preserve your nicer clothes.

80. The cheapest source for quality clothing is a shopaholic friend who shares your size.

81. Clothing items do not have to be worn in just one way. Experiment with different looks and variations to add spice to a simple wardrobe. For instance, long skirts can be worn as dresses or loose tops by placing the waistband above your breasts. Cinch your waistline with a belt to add some definition to your shape. Explore videos on sites like YouTube for ideas.

82. You do not need near as many clothes as you think. Sites like *The Uniform*

Project[4] and *One Dress Protest*[5] are examples of how just a single piece of clothing can be worn.

83. If your closet is bursting at the seams, thin down your wardrobe so that your clothes have some breathing space. Cramming them all together can cause your wardrobe investment to become damaged or wrinkled.

84. If you know how to sew you can convert oversized shirts, pants and dresses to your body shape. There are many videos on YouTube that describe how to do this. This can save a fortune if you have access to free (or nearly free) oversized clothing. Some of the methods do not involve sewing at all. For inspiration you can visit http://newdressaday.wordpress.com/about/.

---

[4] http://www.theuniformproject.com/

[5] http://onedressprotest.com/

85. You can convert worn out jeans into items like handbags, wallets, clutches, laptop bags, shoes and other items. Look online for step by step tutorials that interest you to get the full use out of your old clothing before you discard it.

86. If an item gets stained, dye it a darker color. You can also do this to items that are becoming faded or have started to bore you.

87. If something gets a small tear or loses a button, repair it instead of tossing it in the trash. The longer you can wear an item the more money you save and the kinder you are being to the environment. When you can no longer wear it try to make it into something else.

88. Little kids love to use worn out clothing to make clothes for their dolls. Some

kids will also use those clothes to make new stuff for themselves too.

89. A piece of material (a sheet, curtain or just a random piece of fabric) can be quickly made into a skirt. Sew a single side seam, a bottom hem and a waistband on the top wide enough to hold elastic or a string.

90. Go through your closet and evaluate every item you own at least twice a year; if you find an item that you haven't used lately you can incorporate it into your daily wardrobe for a new look.

91. Place aluminum foil underneath your ironing surface. The foil will conduct the heat better and allow you to iron more efficiently by heating both sides of your garment at once.

92. Use small safety pins to pin hems on pants that are too long.

93. Give new life to your favorite old t-shirt by sewing the openings closed and creating a pillow for your little ones. They will love being able to snuggle up to their Mommy or Daddy doll at night.

94. Use cardboard to make shoe insoles if your soles are thin. My father used cardboard on a pair of leather-soled boots to extend the life of his soles when I was a child.

95. Purchase children's clothing and shoes a size larger than needed. They will be able to wear them even longer before outgrowing them.

96. Line dry your clothes to make them last longer. Modern clothes dryers damage fabrics with the heat and tumbling action. The lint on your dryer screen is actually pieces of fabric stripped off by your dryer.

97. Avoid using dryer balls; they shorten the life of your clothes. The tumbling

action damages the fabric because they literally beat your clothes to death.

98. Turn your denim jeans inside-out before washing them to help preserve the face of the denim and make them last longer.

99. Chip Berg, CEO of Levi Strauss and Co. instructs people to stop washing their jeans if they want to maximize the life of this fashion mainstay. He says to stick them into the freezer overnight to kill germs instead[6].

---

[6] Here is a link to his statement: **http://mashable.com/2014/05/20/levi-ceo-jeans-washing/**

Computers

100. Refill inkjet cartridges instead of purchasing new every time. Make sure you refill them before they run out for best results.

101. Purchase recycled ink cartridges to save money if you don't want to refill them by hand.

102. Sometimes it is cheaper to purchase a whole new printer when the ink cartridges die. Check your prices to

discover if this is the case with your particular printer.

103. Print on draft mode to save on the ink that you use.

104. If you print a lot, invest in a printer that prints on both sides of the paper to save money and trees.

105. Laser printers will save you money if you print a lot. The monochrome ones cost about the same as an inkjet printer these days but the toner cartridges last a *lot* longer.

106. If you only print occasionally and have your inkjet cartridges dry up before you use them up, switch to a laser printer. The toner will last forever with no worries about it going bad.

107. Reuse paper that is printed on only one side: place an X on the used side

and run it through the printer again for non-important printouts.

108. Reuse paper that is printed on only one side for notepaper or let your children use it to create artwork.

109. Avoid serif fonts to reduce the amount of ink you use when you print. Serif fonts are the fonts with the little trailing tips at the end of the letters. Sans serif fonts don't have those little trailing tips. They use less ink when you print as a result.

110. Avoid using dark, heavy & bold fonts in items that you are going to print out. Use fonts with a lighter line like Arial and Calibri.

111. Instead of printing out papers send them to programs like Microsoft OneNote so that you can review, highlight and make notes in them without having to use any paper at all.

112. Invest in a tablet device so that you can eliminate having to use paper notepads. You can hand-write grocery lists, journal entries and even draw with one of these devices.

113. Refurbished Apple computers[7] give you the most bang for your buck as far as computers go these days. They are not only fast, reliable and durable, you don't have to worry about catching a virus and their operating system upgrades are cheap ($20) or free (as in the case of the current Mavericks upgrade). I have to eat some humble pie on this tip because I swore that I would *never* consider switching to an Apple device. After using one and running the numbers I have switched to all-Apple devices for my family.

---

[7] Here's a link directly to Apple's refurbished selection. The offerings change depending upon what is available. **http://store.apple.com/us/browse/home/specialdeals/mac**

114. Use open source software like OpenOffice, Gimp, Audacity, Linux and others for free instead of paying for commercial software solutions.

115. Use the Print Preview feature of your printer so that you can select to print only those pages you need. This will save a lot of ink and paper if you frequently print out web pages. Better yet, don't print those pages out at all for maximum savings.

116. Upgrade your computer instead of buying a new one. A stick of memory does wonders for just a few dollars.

117. Purchase the best computer you can afford when you buy. Doing this will extend the life of the machine because it will have the resources to handle upgrades as they come along for a longer period of time.

118. Do you need both a laptop and a desktop computer? More and more

people are discovering that they can do everything they want on a laptop alone. If you need or want to use a bigger screen or full-size keyboard, connect your laptop to a monitor and regular keyboard instead of investing in a desktop computer.

119. Many people are discovering that their smartphone, tablet (Android or iOS) or iPod Touch completely eliminates their need for a computer. My daughter wrote her school papers on an iPod Touch for a year but has now upgraded to an iPad mini for the larger screen size. I ran my website and writing business from an iPad mini personally for over a year until I could replace the computer I sold when my daughter was very ill. These devices have become so powerful that you may not need a computer at all.

120. Waysale.com[8] offers legitimate copies of Microsoft Office, Microsoft Windows and other software at prices I've not seen beaten anywhere else.

121. Apple offers their iWork and iLife software suites for free on new and refurbished computers, iPads, iPhones and iPod Touches. You won't have to buy an Office Software program at all if you go this route.

122. Computers are now able to replace a number of devices that our parents considered essential. I use my computer to replace my television, my stereo system, my cell phone (I use Google Voice while out for talking and texting) and other items. By taking advantage of all the things your computer can do you can save both money and space in your home.

---

[8] http://www.waysale.com/computers_and_office.html?filter=%26fl3%3D5

123. According to an Apple representative, keyboard and case covers can actually shorten the life of your Apple laptop - in some cases, drastically. The representative explained that Apple uses aluminum casings to wick heat away from sensitive internal components and uses the gaps between the keys on the keyboards to expel heat as well. Covering your Apple laptop with cases and keyboard covers impedes the ability of your laptop to release heat. This causes them to run hotter and thus shortens the life of your computer.

124. According to an Apple representative, encasing your iPad, iPod or iPhone in a protective case may cause your device to overheat and shorten its life - especially if the device sees heavy use. See the previous tip for an explanation of this.

125. When your old computer dies, remove the hard drive and place it inside an external case. This not only allows you to retrieve your files without hiring a data recovery specialist, it gives you an external hard drive on the cheap. Cases for laptop hard drives can be found for as little as $5 on eBay and the hard drives are extremely easy to install, in many cases without requiring any tools. I've done this successfully for years whenever I had a computer die or recycled a dead one for spare parts.

126. Try to stay within a single laptop line when buying laptops for your family or business. This way you may be able to use the broken ones for spare parts as they fail.

127. Don't toss your laptop if the keyboard fails; they are easy and inexpensive to replace. Many after-market keyboards can be found on eBay for less than $20

and can be swapped out in a manner of minutes. Search YouTube for video tutorials featuring your particular laptop.

Entertainment

128. Instead of a television that everyone fights over invest in a tablet or laptop for each member of your household. It will be cheaper than one or more televisions and you won't need a cable subscription.

129. Read books instead of watching television.

130. Instead of buying a stereo use your computer. Modern media players allow you to create playlists, stream

internet radio and (with a laptop) take your music with you.

131. If you purchase a lot of music every month you may save money by subscribing to Spotify[9]. They work a lot like Netflix in that they charge you a monthly fee for access to a large music library.

132. If you read a lot of books companies like Oyster[10], Scribd[11], and Amazon now offer subscription services that allow you to read as many books as you want.

133. Instead of buying a portable DVD player use your laptop. Works just as well and is useful for many other things (like phones, chatting, game playing and reading books).

---

[9] https://www.spotify.com

[10] https://www.oysterbooks.com

[11] http://www.scribd.com

134. Instead of buying a set-top DVD player use your computer. Why buy something new when you already own a computer that can do it?

135. Instead of buying or renting DVDs watch streamed movies on your computer via the Internet. Subscription services like Hulu and Amazon Prime are both safe and much cheaper than buying new. You can even watch stuff online for free[12] if you want.

136. Instead of buying DVD movies check them out at your local library for free. You can do the same with CDs as well.

137. Organize a CD/DVD swap with friends to explore new music and movies without spending more money.

---

[12] **http://annienygma.com/watch_movies_free.htm**

138. Instead of buying books, music or movies check them out at the library for free.

139. Download an ebook reader to your computer. Thousands of classic and modern ebooks are available for free online so you can read as much as you like without having to spend a penny. You may never buy a physical book again.

140. Cancel your cable television subscription and use your computer to watch your favorite television shows.

141. Portable media players are luxuries. Use a netbook, laptop or tablet instead.

142. Use a cassette adapter in older cars to play MP3 music stored on your netbook or laptop. This saves you from having to convert it to cassette tape.

143. Use an FM transmitter to listen to MP3s in a vehicle if it is equipped with a CD player. This is cheaper and faster than burning all of those CDs or buying a new stereo for your car.

144. Choose games that are available for computers instead of investing in expensive (and quickly obsolete) game machines. This will enable you to use a device you already own while saving a fortune on specialized games that aren't compatible with any other device.

145. Instead of buying new video games check out Pawn shops, thrift stores, Craigslist, yard sales and libraries.

146. A large number of local communities have theatre and other entertainment available for free or low cost. Take advantage of them to get out of the house on a shoestring. Join a local

theatre group if you want to be part of the fun.

147. Take turns reading books out loud with your children. This will open their minds to fun adventures and give you memories you will never forget.

148. Play cards, charades and other games with friends and family members instead of investing in video games.

149. Netflix only costs $8 $9[13] a month for unlimited streaming. You and your family can watch whatever you want for way less than a cable subscription.

150. Cancel paper magazine and newspaper subscriptions and read the news online for free. You will help the environment by reducing the amount of trees killed as well with this step.

---

[13] Netflix raised the price for new subscribers in 2014.

151. If you must buy books, CDs and DVDs buy them used instead of new.

Finance

152. If you can't afford to pay cash for an item, don't buy it. Wait until you can actually afford the item.

153. Never rent an item to own. You will pay 2-3 times more compared to buying it with cash.

154. Do not use credit cards, period. Use a bank card as a credit card instead. This will not only save interest charges but will allow you to avoid those ridiculous annual fees.

155. Do not do business with banks that charge monthly maintenance fees. Why should you pay to let them use YOUR money?

156. Avoid ATMs whenever possible to avoid those fees.

157. Don't ever let a waitress or other person remove a credit card from your sight. They could swipe the card with a portable reader and steal your financial information.

158. Don't do financial transactions while connected to public Internet. The internet connection could be hacked and your private bank information stolen.

159. Don't ever reveal personal information to a caller regardless of who they identify themselves to be. Phishers commonly call people and offer special offers for a nominal fee; they then take your credit card

number (or your check account number) and empty your bank account.

160. Make sure you know exactly what services your bank charges extra fees for. Avoid those services.

161. Don't play the lottery. The odds of winning big are almost nonexistent compared to how many people actually play. Drop that dollar into a savings account for an instant win instead.

162. Evaluate every penny you spend; reduce this amount by canceling unused memberships, eliminating unused cable channels, canceling unused subscriptions and any automatic charges that you no longer need but are still paying for.

163. Don't buy out of habit. Just because you grab a new pack of gum every week doesn't mean that you need that

pack. Skip a week once in a while to save a buck.

164. Use online bill pay to save on postage fees and checks.

165. Stay out of stores when you are bored or hungry.

166. If you're single, stay single. Marriages are NOT cheap, especially if you find yourself saddled with a spendthrift.

167. If you're married try to stay that way. Divorces can cost more than marriages do.

168. Don't have kids. I have kids and love them dearly but kids are NOT cheap. Any list of frugal living tips would not be complete without this one admonition. Even if you don't raise them personally the child support could ruin you.

169. Work at home[14] when you can. You will save gas, wear and tear on your vehicle and eliminate the need to own a special wardrobe. Better yet you can spend the day in your pajamas.

170. Live as close to work as possible. If you can walk to work you will save a fortune in gasoline.

171. Don't pay a machine to count your change. Ask your bank for coin wrappers and roll it yourself.

172. Put your unused change in a container instead of keeping it in your pocket. This will reduce the temptation at vending machines and allow you to save money (literally) as well.

173. If you have to drive to work try to carpool with a friend to save money on gas.

---

[14] **https://www.smashwords.com/books/view/36433**

174. Invest your savings into FDIC-insured accounts. This way you are guaranteed by the United States Federal Government not to lose your money. Stocks, bonds, futures and other investments don't have that protection. Why gamble with money you can't afford to lose?

175. If you don't plan to pull money out of your savings for some time, consider US savings bonds. You don't pay taxes on the interest until the bond matures or you redeem it, whichever comes first.

176. If you have debt, eliminate it. Pay it off, file bankruptcy--do whatever you have to do to get out from under the mountain of interest you are paying and then NEVER do it again.

177. Pay your bills on time. Those late fees can cost a sizable chunk!

178. Avoid hanging out with spendthrift friends. They think it as their duty to separate you from your cash.

179. Create a 30-day waiting list for desired purchases. Chances are, after a month, you will no longer want the item in question. This has saved me a fortune by eliminating impulse purchases, especially with my kids.

180. Keep a savings account stashed away for emergencies. This will be the fund you draw from instead of using a credit card. Pay it back with interest every time you borrow from it so that it will be there (and even larger) for the next time.

181. If you have trouble saving money, increase the withholding on your paycheck so that you will receive a nice refund every spring. You can then use that refund to add a large chunk

to your savings or purchase big ticket items.

182. If you have trouble saving money, ask your employer to automatically deduct some money out of your paycheck to go into a savings account. This way you are able to save without having the pain of putting that money away - it is gone before you ever see your paycheck.

183. If you have the time, itemize your deductions when you file your taxes.

184. If your deductions are less than the standard deduction on your tax return just take the standard and save time.

185. Don't brag to your neighbors about the neat stuff you have or the money you keep at home. Don't advertise it by wearing glitzy jewelry or owning an ostentatious vehicle. In tough economic times they **will** burglarize your home and rob you blind.

186. Dress simply and drive a plain older car. Carjackers and auto thieves target the fancy new ones over clunkers and pickpockets will think you're broke and leave you alone.

187. Be willing to try new and zany things. You may discover a new way to save money.

Food

188. Make pizza at home: Take a flour tortilla and spread a light coating of pizza or spaghetti sauce on the surface. Add a thin layer of mozzarella cheese (any cheese will do in a pinch) then add your favorite toppings. Heat in an oven at 400 degrees until the cheese melts and the toppings are cooked through (5-7 minutes in a toaster oven). I cook mine directly on the rack in my toaster oven for a crisp crust. This is cheaper,

fresher, healthier and just as fast as either store-bought or restaurant pizzas. It also enables you to customize the toppings to personal preference instead of using a "one-type-fits-all" approach.

189. No tortilla for your pizza? Line a baking sheet with thin or woven wheat crackers for the crust. This makes a great finger food for kids. I've even used Ritz and Town House crackers for this with no complaints.

190. Cheap is a waste of money if your family won't eat it. Try generic or off-brand items but don't decide to switch unless you family actually likes it.

191. Take your lunch with you to work or school. Eating out for lunch every day is incredibly expensive.

192. Invest in a thermos and brew your own coffee. Learning how to make

premium coffees can eliminate those expensive trips to the coffeehouses.

193. Store leftover coffee in your refrigerator if you don't finish the pot. Microwave by the cup to reheat.

194. Invest in a water filter so that you can stop purchasing bottled water. Carry a water bottle filled with filtered water so that you always have a healthy (and free) drink available. This will save you a fortune by allowing you to bypass the soft drink machine.

195. Always order water when you visit a restaurant. Water is mostly free and much healthier than soft drinks.

196. Leftovers can be used in other items; biscuits can be crumbled and made into bread pudding; cooked meats can become meat salads, sandwiches and other items.

197. To keep a large amount of cool water for a trip freeze a gallon jug of water. Set at room temperature a few minutes before you need it. It will gradually melt, giving you ice cold drinking water throughout the day.

198. If you insist on drinking alcohol, buy the cheap stuff[15].

199. Stale bread can be toasted instead of tossed. The recipient won't be able to tell the difference.

200. Stale bread can be used in French toast.

201. Milk past its prime (slightly soured) can be used instead of fresh or buttermilk in breads and biscuits.

202. Hard cheese with a patch of mold on one end can be saved if you just cut

---

[15] **http://youhavemorethanyouthink.org/10-frugal-ways-to-save-big-on-booze/**

off the bad end[16] with a generous margin. We did this routinely when I was a child and nobody ever got sick from it.

203. Most meat is placed on clearance because it is coming close to the date when stores are no longer allowed to sell it. The meat will not instantly turn bad on that date - you will actually have a few days before the meat turns. For the best price on meat, buy those placed on clearance and freeze until you are ready to eat it.

204. Crackers, cereals and other dry goods contain a small amount of oil that will turn rancid if you try to store them for long periods. As a result you will waste money if you attempt to stockpile these items. Don't buy more than you can use in a couple of

---

[16] **http://www.mayoclinic.org/healthy-living/ nutrition-and-healthy-eating/expert-answers/ food-and-nutrition/faq-20058492**

months to avoid having to throw rancid items away.

205. Place bay leaves in your flour and corn meal to help prevent mealy bugs.

206. Store flour and corn meal in the freezer to help prevent mealy bugs and to keep it fresh longer.

207. Buy bread on sale and store it in the freezer until you need it.

208. Buy edible wheat berries in bulk (white ones have a milder taste than red) then grind to make fresh, whole wheat flour. The unground berries will keep for ages and you will be able to have REAL fresh flour on demand. Coffee grinders and blenders can be used by pulsing to grind them if you don't have a regular flour mill. This flour tastes better than anything you can find in a store.

209. Make your own soymilk. You can buy the soybeans and make it yourself for considerably less than it costs in a grocery store - minus any preservatives and unwanted chemicals. This stuff even costs less than cow's milk if you make it at home[17].

210. If you catch milk on sale, stock up and freeze it[18] until you need it to avoid waste.

211. When cooking rice, soak the rice for 15-30 minutes to reduce the cooking time. Drain this water to reduce the starchy flavor and replace with clear water at a ratio of 2 parts water to 1 part rice.

212. Cook rice on the stove using very little energy. Place your ratio of rice and

---

[17] See the appendix for details.

[18] http://frugalliving.about.com/od/foodsavings/tp/I_Can_Freeze_That.htm

water into a heavy covered pot along with butter and seasonings (optional). When it starts to boil immediately turn off the heat and cover (leave it on the burner - the heat from the burner will continue cooking the rice). Wait 10-12 minutes and fluff with a fork.

213. Hard boil eggs using very little energy. Heat the eggs and water to a rolling boil in a heavy covered pot and then turn off the heat and wait for ten minutes. The residual heat from the burner, the pot and the water will cook the eggs to hard-boiled perfection.

214. Have your meals revolve around a few staples. For instance, our standby meal is baked potatoes: Wash, puncture with a knife, stick in the microwave and hit the "potato" button (6 minutes per potato). Add toppings and enjoy. We also enjoy this standby along with meats and other sides.

215. Reduce the amount of meat that you cook and eat. Instead of a huge piece of meat per person a small slice will do. Add extra vegetables to compensate. You will still have the taste of meat but at a lower cost (because of less meat used) and the added vegetables will make the meal healthier. If you can go meatless on occasion your food bill will really decrease.

216. If you eat a lot of meat, invest in a chest freezer and purchase a quarter, half, or whole animal from your local slaughterhouse. They will package it to suit you and you will save a fortune over buying the meat in the store.

217. Make your own frozen dinners. Cook a large meal and portion out on paper plates (I prefer the 3-compartment plates for this). Stick each plate in a freezer bag, date and freeze. Microwave when you need a quick

meal. If you have three-compartment lunch containers, use those instead to save even more money over buying paper plates.

218. Prepare only as much food as your family will eat for that meal. You will save a fortune in discarded leftovers.

219. Limit bringing soft drinks home to an occasional treat. Drink water instead.

220. Invest in an electric kettle if you frequently heat water for drinks. They heat water *much* faster and use considerably less energy over the stovetop.

221. Easy Ramen prep: Place ramen noodles in a bowl, pour enough boiling water over them to completely cover them and cover the bowl with a heavy plate or a lid. Wait five minutes and stir for perfect noodles without the fuss. This uses less energy than boiling the noodles on the stove.

Experiment with water levels if you prefer less or more water in your ramen noodles.

222. Store almost-empty condiment bottles upside down in the refrigerator to get the last drop out.

223. Invest in a chest freezer. You can buy meats and other foods in bulk at lower prices (or on sale) and then freeze until you are ready to eat them.

224. Go grocery shopping while in a hurry. You won't be tempted to browse as much.

225. Always use a list when grocery shopping. Don't allow yourself to vary from the list.

226. Keep track of expiration dates on food. Use or freeze items before they spoil to prevent wasting money.

227. Make your own baby food[19]. It will be cheaper by far and healthier besides.

228. Use a heavy-duty paper clamp or a clothespin to close bags of chips when you're done eating them. This helps them to stay fresh longer.

229. To freshen stale chips, place in a single layer on a paper towel and microwave for 30 seconds. Allow to cool then test. If they still taste stale microwave them for 30 seconds more. This removes the moisture that makes them taste stale.

230. Rehydrate wilted vegetables like celery, lettuce and spinach by soaking in cold water for a few minutes. Dry well when finished.

231. Explore new recipes from websites like the One Dollar Diet Project[20]. You

---

[19] http://littlelovely.typepad.com/littlelovely/2009/12/how-to-make-your-own-baby-food.html

[20] http://onedollardietproject.wordpress.com/

may find some new favorite meals and save money in the process.

232. When shopping for groceries know that you don't have to buy all 5 items to get the $5 dollar price in 5 for $5 sales. The prices are calculated by computerized cash registers and they will be programmed to charge $1 per item.

233. When you make a large batch of dried beans use the leftovers to make refried beans and get more use out of the meal.

234. When making tacos or burritos cut the amount of ground meat in half and substitute refried beans in the recipe. It will taste just as well and cost a lot less.

235. Rabbits can be raised in most urban environments as an inexpensive meat. Give them lots of fresh clover and grass clippings to reduce the feed

expense. You may have to give them names and call them pets to the neighbors, however.

236. Grow herbs on your windowsill for fresh herbs on the cheap.

Gardening

237. Shredded newspaper can be used as mulch around garden plants.

238. Grass clippings can be used as mulch for garden plants.

239. Crush egg shells and use in your garden to provide your plants with much-needed calcium.

240. Used coffee grounds and tea leaves can be sprinkled around plants to help fertilize them naturally.

241. Pour leftover coffee and tea (no cream or sugar, please!) around plants to help fertilize them naturally.

242. Pour discarded aquarium water around plants for a natural fertilizer.

243. Start cuttings by placing them in a glass of aquarium water. They will root faster. I have seen people successfully grow pothos simply by sticking the roots into their aquarium and letting the vines hang along the outside. The plant was gorgeously lush!

244. Mow over dead leaves instead of raking them up. The leaves will decompose and provide a natural fertilizer for the soil.

245. Use a mulching lawn mower and do not remove grass clippings from your yard. The clippings will fertilize the soil for free.

246. Water your house and garden plants with the water you drain from your pasta.

247. Place a rain barrel beneath your gutter's downspout. Use this to water your garden for free.

248. Trade plant clippings with a friend to expand your houseplant collection.

249. When planting outside flowers, use perennials so that they will grow back every year.

250. Some annuals like sunflowers will reseed themselves and come back every year. You can choose to save the seeds or simply allow them to reseed themselves.

251. Grow perennial flowers in your garden to decorate your home with instead of purchasing the cut variety. Clip and display during the flowering season.

General Household

252. Store candles in the freezer. They will burn better and last longer.

253. If you find yourself needing a tool, appliance or other item temporarily borrow one from a friend instead of buying it.

254. If you have an appliance suddenly fail, rent one for a week while you shop for a replacement to avoid spending more because you are desperate.

255. Front-loading washing machines use significantly less water than top loading machines. If you do a lot of laundry this can save you a fortune over time.

256. If you are considering the purchase of a particular high-dollar item, rent one first to make sure that it will suit your needs before you spend the money to buy one.

257. If you are moving house; sell, toss or otherwise eliminate as much of your furniture as possible to minimize your moving expense.

258. If your furniture and appliances are very old it may be cheaper to replace them than to move them with you when you switch homes.

259. Unwrap your bar soaps when you get them home and store them in a dry place until you use them. This will allow them to dry out and they will

last considerably longer. In fact, the longer you let them "cure" this way, the better.

260. Dilute your shampoos and dishwashing liquids half-and-half with water. They will clean just as well as full-strength.

261. Cut an inch off of the bottom of your Christmas tree before you use it. This helps the tree take up water better so that it will last longer.

262. If you have mice and insect problems consider investing in a cat. They will rid your home of mice and some insects naturally. It is even claimed that cats will hunt down and kill roaches[21]; I have personally seen my cat kill not only roaches but spiders, crickets and other insects.

---

[21] http://www.squidoo.com/howtokillroaches

263. One of the best ways to eliminate roaches is to use the roach bait that comes in tubes like Max Force roach gel. Place small dabs of this gel everywhere you see roaches like behind picture frames, under cabinet drawers, underneath your kitchen table, within kitchen counters, above window and door frames and other out of the way places roaches love to hide. The results won't be instant but the critters *will* die. This works better than anything else I have used and is much cheaper than an exterminator.

264. Chickens and guineas that are allowed free rein will keep the insect population under control in your yard. They also provide eggs and meat for your dinner table as an added bonus.

265. Catnip and bay leaves will help to repel roaches. Scatter the leaves around where roaches travel.

266. When you think you've squeezed the last bit out of a tube, cut it open. You will be amazed at what is left inside.

267. Save aluminum cans and other bits of metal to sell at a recycle center. Every penny adds up!

268. Don't spray or fog a home that is heavily infested with roaches. It will look as if you are living in *Joe's Apartment* if you do. Your family will freak out and demand to be taken to a hotel room if you don't beat them to the car first. Bait your home thoroughly instead to kill them the slow way. Don't ask me how I know this. 😖

269. Don't accept items from people who live in roach-infested homes. Roaches love to hitchhike and they can be expensive to remove.

270. Kill roaches by mixing borax half-and-half with powdered sugar. Sprinkle

around in crevasses and corners just like you would regular boric acid (Roach Prufe).

271. Kill roaches[22] by mixing 1/3 cup borax, 1/3 powdered sugar and 1/3 cup cocoa. Sprinkle around just like Roach Prufe and leave it out for continuous coverage.

272. Kill mice and rats by mixing quick-setting concrete and flour in a pan. Place a pan of water nearby but not close enough to mix with the powder. The mice and rats eat the powder and drink the water. *Note*: this seems cruel but is just as cruel as traditional poisons and much cheaper if you need a lot. Keep away from animals[23].

---

[22] **http://www.straightdope.com/columns/read/20/ whats-the-best-way-to-kill-cockroaches**

[23] For more information and some other rodent tips visit **http://www.listafterlist.com/tabid/57/listid/ 4160/Home++Garden/Pest+Control+Tips +Rodents.aspx**.

273. Spritz roaches with rubbing alcohol for a quick death.

274. Spray roaches with dishwashing liquid to suffocate them. Flush them down the commode to get rid of them before any eggs they are carrying can hatch.

275. If you live in an area that has roach, bedbug or similar insect problems, limit or eliminate the amount of upholstered furniture you own. Insects love to live in upholstery and are almost impossible to remove if your home becomes infested. In some cases (bedbugs, especially) you may even be forced to replace your upholstered furniture at significant expense, whereas unupholstered items will only need to be washed off.

276. If you live in an area that has roach, bedbug or similar problems, cover your mattresses and pillowcases with

protective cases designed to protect against these nasties. This will save you from having to replace these items in the event of an infestation.

277. Avoid purchasing toilet paper by using family cloths instead of bathroom tissue. These cloths are washed and reused instead of bathroom tissue. If you own a washer and hang the cloths to dry it is very economical - especially if you have kids who love using LOTS of toilet paper.

278. Instead of purchasing sanitary napkins for the monthly menstrual cycle use cloths to catch the flow. Folded wash cloths can be soaked in a bucket and then washed after your flow has stopped.

279. Instead of purchasing sanitary pads or tampons you can use a menstrual cup that you remove, rinse and reuse.

280. Bandannas are simply old-fashioned handkerchiefs. Use them instead of facial tissue to blow your nose and pocket the difference. You only need two: wash one and let it drip dry while you are using the other one.

281. Take care of your purchases to make them last as long as possible. This will help prevent having to spend money on replacement items.

282. If your freezer has a musty smell clean well with baking soda and water. Dampen a cotton pad with vanilla extract (not the imitation stuff) and wipe down the walls. It will solve the problem. Alternately you can try soaking a cotton ball in the extract and leaving it in the freezer before you clean it to help with the smell until you have time for a good scrubbing.

283. Give your leftover coffee and tea (minus cream and sugar) to your

plants to provide them with a few extra nutrients on the cheap. Why pour those nutrients down a drain?

284. Make ice for coolers by freezing a gallon jug (or smaller if your cooler is tiny). Place it inside the cooler or smash it with a hammer and sprinkle the ice inside.

285. When your scented candle loses its wick, melt the wax on a candle warmer and use chopsticks to pull the wick out of the melted wax. Remove the candle from heat and watch it as it cools. It will harden from the outside in. When the wax forms an outer circle small enough to support the wick without it falling back in (but the center is still melted) replace the wick. If you wait too long stir the center with the chopstick to loosen a bit. Allow to fully harden and you will have your candle back.

286. If there is a bit of wax left in your scented candle (but your wick has burned up), melt the wax on a candle warmer and pour into an oil or tart burner. You can then use tealight candles to warm the wax and enjoy all of the scent. Alternatively, just keep the candle on the candle warmer for the same effect.

287. Use scented fragrance oil on your cloth when dusting wooden furniture to add scent to a room.

288. Boil citrus peels on the stove to perfume your kitchen. Add a few cloves to the water for a rich aroma.

289. Spread apple peels on a baking sheet and allow to dry in an out of the way spot. As they dry they will release a gentle smell.

290. If you have a small hole in drywall you don't have to buy patching plaster. Just fill the hole with plain

white toothpaste (non-gel) and allow to dry.

291. Reuse coffee cans and jars as storage containers for dried beans, rice, flour and other items.

292. For thin, sheer curtains skip the expense of a curtain rod. Tack them to the top of the windowsill with push pins instead.

293. If you need a curtain in a pinch but don't have a curtain rod, tack or staple a piece of fabric to the top of the windowsill. Start by securing in the center and on each end and then distribute the fabric evenly. This makes a great curtain in a pinch, especially if you staple it with a staple gun and conceal the staples in the fabric folds. Cut it up the center to make it look like two panels and run a bead of super glue across the edges to seal. Voila! Instant curtain!

294. Inexpensive flat sheets make great curtains. Run the curtain rod in the wide hem that is at the top of sheet or tack it to the windowsill if you don't have a curtain rod handy.

295. If you have a really ugly wall where there are holes, peeling paint or whatever, fix it up instantly and cheaply by stapling sheets to it. Ruffle them to make it look like a large closed curtain or add a layer of batting beneath it for a padded look (and extra insulation to the wall). Colorful push pins add character if used to secure the material to a padded wall.

296. Frame attractive pictures from magazines and calendars instead of investing in expensive artwork. You can even print out images that you find on the internet for this.

297. Make a closet in any recess by attaching a heavy rod near the top and

using a curtain mounted on a pressure rod for a door.

298. Go with the smallest appliances you can comfortably use. This will save you money, space and headaches. For instance, instead of a full-size stove and refrigerator in our home we have a 2-burner hot plate, a toaster oven, a microwave, an under counter refrigerator and a small chest freezer. All of these items (except for the chest freezer) are inserted in the space the full-size stove would normally reside, while the refrigerator recess has the chest freezer on the bottom and my closet on top, hidden with a curtain. This allows us to cook and store food comfortably while maximizing the space we have available.

299. Purchase appliances used when possible but make sure it is a good bargain.

300. Sometimes it is better (and cheaper) to purchase a smaller appliance new than a larger one used.

301. Color code keys and other items by painting them with fingernail polish instead of buying key covers.

302. Liquid stitch is essentially super glue; in fact super glue was used by the military as a way to patch wounded soldiers together on the battlefield. If you have a bottle lying around you can use it to repair miscellaneous plastic items as well as small cuts. I wouldn't recommend using a bottle of regular super glue on cuts however; it's a slightly different formulation[24] that may irritate the skin.

303. If something breaks try to repair it before replacing it.

---

[24] http://www.straightdope.com/columns/read/2187/was-super-glue-invented-to-seal-battle-wounds-in-vietnam

304. Avoid using disposable products. Use cloth instead of paper napkins and towels and then toss them into the washer when they're dirty.

305. Buy the cheapest, longest-lasting bathroom tissue you can find. In this area it is the Family Dollar tissue that is the generic equivalent to Scott's tissue (it has more on the rolls). *2014 Update: The Great Value Tissue at WalMart with 1250 sheets in each roll is a slightly better value today compared to the Family Dollar brand.* Why spend a fortune on something you are going to flush down the drain?

306. Buy the cheapest, longest-lasting paper towels you can find. Why spend money on something you are going to use once and throw away?

307. Hang strips of duct tape in fly-infested areas around the home. The flies will stick to the tape just like they would

fly strips and you don't have to worry about your store running out in the cooler months if your kid's science experiment creates a legion of gnats.

308. Store plastic grocery bags in a large gym sock. Hang the sock in your pantry for easy access whenever you need a new trash bag.

309. Reuse shoe boxes to store items in. Cover them with fabric or paint them to match your décor.

310. Old shower curtains make excellent drop cloths for messy projects.

311. Paper egg cartons make great seed starters. Fill with potting soil, start your seeds then separate the sections and plant directly into your garden. The pressed paper will rot and help fertilize your new plant.

312. Paper can be used as a customized funnel for tight spots. Just make the

small end the proper dimension to match the opening you are trying to fill.

313. Heavy paper or thin cardboard can be used as a dustpan. Hold it in one hand and sweep the dirt into it with the other.

314. If you love to paint, cut old hollow core doors to size and tape the edges with masking tape to make a frugal canvas. An art major learned this tip from his instructor, who said that it would save money even if you purchased the doors new.

Housing

315. Secure the smallest square footage that you really need. Smaller is cheaper in the housing market. More people prefer larger to smaller so the premium pricing is on the larger properties.

    The only exception to this would be if you could rent/buy a larger place for significantly less than a smaller one. For instance, while my daughter and I can comfortably live in a 500 square foot 1-bedroom, I jumped on the opportunity to pay cash for a 720 square foot 2 bedroom because it was cheaper to buy the larger place than it was to rent something smaller. Just remember to factor in the added expense of heating and cooling a larger space.

316. A single person can live in an efficiency (studio) apartment while 2-3 can live in a 1 bedroom without issue. The world will not end if your kids have to share a bedroom.

317. You can utilize the Japanese concept of multi-purpose rooms in smaller houses to maximize the space you have. In the mountains where I grew up the parents would sleep on a bed in the living room while the kids piled up several to a bed, with multiple beds per room.

318. Just because a house is designed with a certain room layout doesn't mean you have to use them this way. For instance, my cousin turned her dining room into a living room (her kitchen was large enough for a table) then closed off the official living room to give her family an extra bedroom without the cost of an addition (or larger home). Unconventional thinking can save you a fortune!

319. Pay cash for your home. You will save thousands, if not tens of thousands of dollars this way. This is NOT impossible; I've paid cash for 2 homes now and I know several friends who paid cash for their homes. The trick is to buy what you can honestly afford.

320. In some areas it is much cheaper to rent than it is to purchase, especially if you don't plan to stay forever. Know your local housing market.

321. To double the houses on a lot while sidestepping housing codes, place a Tumbleweed[25] or similar home on a trailer in the backyard. Both buildings can share water and electric hookups while the Tumbleweed can use a composting commode to avoid sewage concerns.

322. Pay extra on your mortgage payment every month. This will pay your principle down MUCH faster and can save you a fortune in interest charges.

323. Windows are a huge source of drafts in a home. Less windows = less hot/cold air that can leak into your home. I've seen apartments and homes with almost no windows and the owners bragged that they were really easy to heat and cool. Some may not be able to handle the lack of sunlight, however.

---

[25] http://www.tumbleweedhouses.com/

324. If you have a fireplace make sure you have a damper installed. You can close this when you're not using the fireplace to prevent your heated air from escaping.

325. Singles and couples may find it cheaper to live in a small RV or a simple van instead of buying a house or paying rent in some parts of the country.

326. Stuff plastic grocery bags in crevasses that allow cold air in your home. Areas to focus on are around water pipes, old windows that have a gap and where the floor meets the wall if your floor is sinking in areas. This is a free insulation you can use when you rent or can't afford to seal the holes properly. I've even used this and newspaper to seal unused ductwork in older homes.

327. If you have a small yard it may be cheaper to pay a neighbor to mow your grass then to buy a mower and do it yourself. You may also be able to trade services with your neighbor and get your yard mowed for free if you ask.

Kids

328. Buy children's clothing a bit larger than they need. This will ensure that they get more use out of it even if they have a growth spurt.

329. Yard sales and thrift shops are excellent places to buy used children's clothing. Kids rarely get full use out of their clothes before growing out of them so most items will be hardly

used, especially since we wear only 20%[26] of the clothing we own.

330. Kids only need 1-2 weeks' worth of clothes. They grow too fast to get the full use out of a larger wardrobe.

331. The more time children spend watching television the more commercials they are exposed to. The more commercials they are exposed to the more stuff they will beg you to buy.

332. Kids need the attention of their parents more than they need stuff.

333. Babies do NOT need every cute thing the store displays. If they are warm, dry, fed and loved they are happy.

334. Place an assortment of dried beans inside of a 2-liter bottle then glue the lid in place. Little ones will roll this around for hours.

---

[26] http://getsimplifized.com/the-80-20-rule

335. Reuse baby wipe containers to store small items. These containers will last and last.

336. Place an old shower curtain on the floor underneath baby's high chair. Shake out, hang on the clothesline and spray off when done to keep your home cleaner.

337. Instead of buying every single electronic device that your teen requests, compromise by purchasing a single device that has multiple uses. For instance, instead of getting my daughter a laptop, a TV, a DVD player, a stereo, a video camera and a game machine we invested in an iPad. She can watch movies online, listen to music, read books, play games, chat with friends, make videos and even do her homework on it, which saved me a fortune.

338. Instead of buying your kid a bunch of cheap gifts that they will never use (and thus are a waste of money), ask them what they *really* want and get that instead. That single item may be a bit more expensive than all of the stuff you would have normally purchased but it will actually get used, increasing the value of the gift. Your kid will also appreciate it a lot more than they will a bunch of stuff they don't want and won't use.

Personal Care

339. Only use a pea-sized amount of toothpaste. Any more is a waste.

340. Dip a damp toothbrush into some baking soda or salt to clean your teeth for practically nothing.

341. To whiten teeth dampen your brush with hydrogen peroxide and dip into baking soda. This is cheaper than buying whitening toothpaste that contains the same ingredients.

342. Sprinkle corn starch under your arms to help absorb odors without dangerous chemicals (and for much less than commercial deodorant).

343. Sprinkle baking soda under your arms to control odors.

344. In the old days baby powder didn't exist. Parents used corn starch to control moisture instead. That is why there are high-dollar containers of baby powder that contain corn starch. Save a fortune by buying the stuff in the food section instead.

345. Dab a few drops of fragrance oil on your pulse points for perfume on the uber-cheap. Rubbing a bit on your hands and then rubbing your hands through your hair will perfume your whole head as well.

346. For maximum cleaning on the cheap, skip the toothpaste and scrub your teeth with a damp toothbrush to

remove built-up plaque and deposits. Rinse your mouth and then brush normally with toothpaste, baking soda or salt.

347. A teaspoon of salt in a cup of water makes an excellent frugal mouth rinse.

348. Rinsing your mouth with plain water is the cheapest method of rinsing out your mouth after you brush your teeth.

349. Gargle with cayenne pepper[27] to help relieve sore throat. It can save an expensive doctor visit.

350. To exfoliate and help with ingrown hairs make a paste of baking soda with water and rub in a circular motion on your skin with a loofah mitt. Rinse well and follow with a moisturizer. This also helps to remove peach fuzz from your skin.

---

[27] http://myfinancialjourney.com/archive/frugal-cure-for-a-sore-throat

351. Use a towel instead of a hair dryer. Both your hair and your wallet will thank you.

352. Choose hair styles that do not require (a) regular trips to the salon, (b) specialty electric appliances like dryers, flat irons, curlers, etc. (c) gels, sprays, colors or other regular purchases.

353. Learn how to French braid your own hair. This classic style always looks gorgeous and is perfect for bad hair days. It also looks more stylish than a ponytail ever will. You can watch videos on YouTube to learn this valuable skill.

354. Practice simple updo hair styles. Buns, braids and other designs are easy to do and always look stylish and attractive on a lady. You can avoid getting your hair cut indefinitely if you master the art of the updo.

355. Tip from a teen: to color the tips of your hair, use one packet of sugar-free Kool-Aid (the one that needs you to add sugar) mixed with a cup of hot water[28]. I am told that this will last longer than commercial colors - and cost a lot less.

356. To bleach your hair for pennies, wet thoroughly with peroxide and allow to dry. Repeat until you reach your desired shade of blonde. *Note:* those with red hues may go through an "orange" stage during the bleaching process. Don't panic - just keep reapplying the peroxide (allowing to dry between treatments) to remove. I have red hues in my hair and bleached my hair successfully using this very method for years. Condition

---

[28] The recipe I was given only used one cup of water, but some online recipes say that you need two. You can find a step-by step tutorial here: http://www.wikihow.com/Dip-Dye-Hair-with-Kool-Aid

your hair well when done, especially if it takes several rounds to get your hair to the desired lightness.

357. Brown hair coloring tends to last a bit longer than reds if you color your hair. For those whose original hair color is dark blonde/light brown (like mine), I've noticed that as it fades the roots won't be as noticeable as it is with blonde, red or black hair color choices. I have no idea about how the roots will show for those with gray hair.

358. Men always look timeless in short, simple cuts though some males look astounding either shaved bald or with long flowing hair. These styles need not cost a fortune; the simplest cuts can be done with a pair of clippers.

359. Clean, well-trimmed fingernails always look gorgeous. Skip the paint and extensions for a beautiful, timeless look.

360. In a pinch just brush your teeth with plain warm water to clean them for almost nothing.

361. If your favorite fingernail polish is down to the dregs you can refresh it for one last coat by adding a few drops of polish remover to the bottle and shaking well.

362. Dab insect bites with pure ammonia to control itching. It is the same ingredient that a lot of anti-itch treatments contain.

363. To relieve the discomfort of insect bites heat the bowl of a spoon under hot water and then place it upon the bite. The heat will kill the enzymes that make you itch.

364. In the old days bee stings were treated by chewing on a piece of tobacco to moisten it and then placing the tobacco piece upon the sting.

365. Sugar poured or packed in a wound will help promote healing. This has been used successfully even on persistent and deep wounds.[29]

366. Washing hands with plain soap and water (taking care to scrub and rinse well) will save a fortune in medical bills if done regularly; especially if done before handling food or touching an open wound.

367. Using daylight-spectrum lighting during the winter months can help with seasonal depression, saving money on medication and therapist visits.

368. Use up those last bits of soap by tossing them in a lone sock and tying the end. Use this to lather and scrub

---

[29] For more information check out the following free PDF: http://www.hungarovet.com/wp-content/uploads/2007/08/wound-management-using-sugar-2002.pdf.

when you bathe and add more soap pieces when they become available.

369. Use up the last bits of soap by attaching them to the new bar. Soften the old bar with water, dampen the new bar and stick them together. This enables you to use every last piece of soap.

370. Add water to shampoo, conditioner or soap bottles and shake well to get the very last dregs out.

371. Quit smoking. This will save you thousands in tobacco products alone, not including how many dollars you will save in medical bills when you quit.

372. Rolling your own cigarettes can save you a fortune if you smoke. You can make both filtered and non-filtered cigarettes (non-filtered is cheaper, of course) in a variety of flavors. A big bag of tobacco costs about the same as

two packs of cigarettes and will make about two cartons.

373. E-cigarettes are considerably less expensive than regular cigarettes, especially if you refill the cartridges. A five pack of cartridges (the equivalent of five packs of cigarettes) costs around $10 - less than half the price. When you refill those cartridges it reduces the price even more.

374. Drink in moderation or not at all. Not drinking alcohol is the cheapest method.

375. If you do drink, don't drive. Not only do you endanger other people's lives when you drive intoxicated but you run the risk of expensive tickets, attorney's fees, losing your license and possibly your job - besides the fact that you could kill someone.

376. Learn how to cut your own hair. For really short cuts purchase a pair of

clippers and cut it yourself. Longer hair styles can be trimmed yourself as well. Just avoid the high-maintenance styles and opt for classic, easy to trim looks.

377. Keep disposable razors clean and dry to extend their life. Rub the blades back and forth along a piece of denim to help sharpen the blades[30]; the recommended number of up and down strokes is 20. Store your blades in a cup of rubbing alcohol to ensure that moisture will not rust the blade between uses (it will also help prevent germ buildup).

378. Dry your razor blades after each use to extend the life of your blades.

379. Purchase an old-fashioned double-edged safety razor from a thrift shop or online and refill it instead of buying

---

[30] http://www.instructables.com/id/How-to-extend-the-life-of-your-Razor-Blade-keeping/

disposables. The blades tend to last much longer than the ones on disposable razors and the overall expense is considerably less. I bought my safety razor for a couple of dollars on Amazon and the blades cost a dollar for a ten pack at local stores.

380. Create your own liquid soap[31] by melting down bar soap at a cost of pennies. Grate a half of a bar of your favorite soap. Heat it on the stove (medium temperature) with a quart of water, stirring until the soap has completely dissolved. Pour into a gallon container and top off with cool water. Shake well before use and use to refill your liquid soap dispensers.

381. If your family members insist on using several pumps of liquid soap when they wash their hands, dilute the liquid soap half and half with

---

[31] See appendix for details.

water. They will get the proper amount of soap without the waste.

382. Create foaming soap by diluting liquid soap. Pour 1/2 inch of liquid soap into the bottom of a foaming soap dispenser. Add water until you reach the fill mark, cap and shake well. Some soaps may need a thicker or thinner dilution so experiment until you reach the right combination for your favorite brand. This will save you a fortune if you love using the foaming soap (or even liquid soap because it is highly diluted).

383. Don't skimp on sleep. Let your body rest when it is tired because a tired body is more prone to illness and injury. Medical bills aren't cheap.

384. Always use protection when you have sex. sexually transmitted diseases run the gamut from being expensive to impossible to cure. It will also help to

prevent unwanted (and expensive) pregnancies. Celibacy is the safest (and cheapest) method but isn't very common anymore.

385. If you need medication purchase generics. Do this for both prescription and over the counter medications.

386. Do not allow your doctor to prescribe you medications if there is a more natural treatment available. For instance, high blood pressure and diabetes can sometimes be treated with diet changes. Talk to your doctor about trying these first before you spend your money.

387. Use mineral oil, petroleum jelly or olive oil to moisturize your skin instead of paying for expensive lotions.

388. If your hands or feet are really dry, rub well with petroleum jelly, cover with socks (cloth gloves if for hands)

and go to bed. The skin will be softer by morning.

389. Eliminate using shampoo entirely by mixing a teaspoon of baking soda in a cup of warm water. Massage through your hair and scalp, then rinse. You will be amazed at the gunk this simple no-lather cleaner removes!

390. If you have to go to a doctor ask for a discount if you pay cash. If he quibbles remind him that he won't have to spend a fortune filing a claim and then wait for months in hopes that an insurance company will finally pay him.

391. Tiger Balm (red or white) helps repel mosquitoes and soothes the itch of stings. Dab on your stings and on pulse points, or lightly rub some on exposed areas of your skin for maximum effectiveness.

392. Condoms are offered for free in some health departments and are sometimes left in the restrooms of businesses. Use these instead of buying them.

393. Tip from a doctor: Cover warts with duct tape for 6 days. Remove the tape then soak the wart in water and scrub with a pumice stone. If portions of the wart remain after this, reapply the tape for 6 more days and repeat.

394. Use a clean cotton pad (or gauze pad) and a piece of duct tape for a cheap band-aid that will actually stay put. Choose a pretty color or pattern of duct tape for the kids.

395. Wrap duct tape around the cuffs of your pants when hiking in wooded areas. This will help prevent chiggers from getting to your ankles and help avoid the use of anti-itch creams.

396. Grave sites are expensive. Help your survivors save money by requesting that your remains be cremated and scattered somewhere. This saves the expense of a burial plot and a headstone for the grieving family.

397. Avoid the cost of cremation entirely by donating your body to science. They will cremate your body for free and either return the ashes to your family or offer the option of having the remains scattered at sea. You can help medical science and save your family money at the same time.

398. Instead of an expensive funeral hosted at a funeral home have a memorial service hosted at a park, church or other public venue.

399. If your teeth are in very poor condition and require multiple expensive procedures you may save money, improve your health and

eliminate your pain by just having the teeth in question pulled and replaced with false teeth.

400. Always use a soft-bristled toothbrush when cleaning your teeth. Harder bristles can damage the enamel and lead to tooth decay.

401. Avoid drinking soft drinks. Soft drinks have a high acid content that can damage your teeth, causing the need for expensive dental procedures. Think about it: if a soft drink can remove corrosion on a battery and remove hard water stains in a commode, what is it doing to your teeth?

402. Instead of buying expensive dry shampoos rub oatmeal or corn starch into your hair and then brush out well.

403. Make a batch of ginger candy[32] and suck on a piece whenever your stomach is upset instead of buying expensive medicine.

404. Add a teaspoon of baking soda to a glass of water and drink to cure eggy burps on the cheap.

405. Drink dill pickle juice to help with the occasional bout of diarrhea.[33]

406. If you have trouble falling asleep, dim the lights, turn off the TV, computer or tablet and curl up with a soothing physical book (not an ebook!) for about an hour before bed. This allows your internal clock to reset itself for bedtime and may save you from having to take expensive sleeping pills.

---

[32] See the appendix for the recipe.

[33] It also helps with dairy intolerance. See the appendix for details.

Pets

407. Adopt a cat or kitten at the local animal shelter during "Adopt a Cat Month." (normally in June). The adoption fee will be significantly less during this month. You will save the life of a cat or kitten, get that same animal spayed or neutered along with shots for MUCH less than if you were to pay full-price for the services and you will have an animal that will serve as a natural form of pest control, killing mice and insects. They also have a similar special for dogs.

408. Adopt a dog or a cat instead of getting a "free" animal. The adoption fee will be considerably less than if you pay personally to have a vet exam, shots and spay/neuter done on an animal you have been given. You will also have the pleasure of knowing that you saved an animal's life.

409. Small pets like hamsters, rabbits, guinea pigs and birds can cost big money. Cages, feed, bed lining, treats and other items can quickly get expensive. They also require a lot more maintenance then one would expect. Consider well before investing in one of these animals.

410. Animal rescue workers have told me they use Sevin Dust as flea powder[34] on cats, dogs, squirrels, rabbits and other animals. It is what their vet recommended. You can also use this

---

[34] **http://extension.umaine.edu/ipm/ipddl/ publications/5020e/**

dust in your yard[35] to help control fleas and other insects as well.

411. Save a vet visit: if you suspect that your pet is suffering from ringworm, examine the area with a black light. The black light will cause ringworms to glow for an easy diagnosis. This works on humans as well.

412. If your pet is suffering from ringworm, treat for ten days with an OTC anti-fungal medication such as that marketed for athlete's foot. This works for humans as well.

413. Heartworm medicine savings: Dog rescue organizations inform me that they save money on heartworm preventative by purchasing Advantage Multi in the largest available size and then dosing according to the dog's weight. They use 1 ml. per 22 pounds of weight to

---

[35] http://neuro.vetmed.ufl.edu/neuro/fleas.htm

treat their rescued dogs for fleas, heartworms and other intestinal worms.

414. Sprinkle borax on carpets and sweep in to help control fleas. Reapply every time you vacuum. By keeping it applied it will break the life cycle of the insect and kill any new ones that come in on your pets.

415. Buying pet food in bulk is not wise if the food will go stale before your pet eats it. Only purchase what your animals will eat in a month or so.

416. Shredded paper can be used instead of wood chips if it is not coated in toxic inks in the cages of small animals.

417. Make an aquarium cleaning siphon using a 2-liter bottle and a piece of a garden hose. Cut the bottom off of the bottle and attach the top to the water hose. Use like a normal aquarium

siphon cleaner. Insert a small piece of screen where the hose connects to the bottle if you are worried that gravel will be sucked out of the aquarium.

418. Instead of purchasing an expensive aquarium lid use two inexpensive clamp-on desk lights and equip with bulbs. Mount them to the sides of the tank and focus the light on the fish. This is much cheaper than purchasing a hood for lighting.

419. If you are worried about animals bothering your aquarium create a lid by using household screening. Thin boards can be used to make a frame that will fit on top of your particular aquarium to keep out unwanted animals.

420. Cold-water fish are less expensive to keep than tropical fish because they do not require a heater for warmth. Therefore you are saved the expense

of purchasing the heater and the electric needed to operate it.

421. The smaller the dog, the less it eats.

422. Small, yappy dogs make great alarm systems. Burglars hate to break into houses with noisy dogs.

423. Bag Balm is an excellent salve to rub on animal injuries. I once used this to heal a dog that had been stabbed under the chin by a gas thief. The wound healed completely without a vet visit.

424. Pet treats can be made at home[36] easily and inexpensively.

425. Non-upholstered furniture is best for homes with pets. It is long lasting, easy to clean and can't harbor fleas and other insects. This also applies to homes with small kids as well.

---

[36] See appendix for a simple pet treat recipe.

426. Small dogs can easily ride with you on airplane, bus or train trips which will allow you to avoid costly boarding fees. You can put them in one of those purse-like carriers and go.

427. Bathe and groom your pets yourself. You will develop a closer bond with the animal and save a fortune in grooming fees.

428. Dawn Dishwashing liquid is a frugal, gentle alternative to pet flea shampoo according to some vets. Lather up, allow to sit for a few minutes and then rinse well. This is all I use to bathe my pets now and it works really well.

429. Make pet toys instead of buying them. Place a tennis ball into a sport sock and tie the open end, or braid strips of discarded blue jeans and knot both ends to make a tug rope. Use plastic container lids for Frisbees. The possibilities are endless - and much

cheaper than what you will find at a store.

430. Yard sale and thrift shop stuffed animals (minus pieces that pets can choke on like eye buttons) are a delight to pups and older dogs alike. Why pay $$ when you can get them for pennies?

431. Bathroom tissue tubes make delightful tunnels for hamsters and gerbils.

432. Guinea pigs love having a small cardboard box "house" they can hide in and chew on. Instead of buying one of the specialty houses just give them a little box.

433. Guinea pigs love to eat grass, clover and other plants. Pull some out of the yard for a free and tasty treat for your furry friend.

434. Let your guinea pig have first chance at your vegetable scraps. Remove any

leftovers before bedtime to avoid attracting insects.

435. Have your pets spayed or neutered. This saves money on pet food, vet bills (neutered animals stay healthier) and the expense of finding homes for the babies.

436. Keep small animals (gerbils, hamsters, guinea pigs, rabbits, etc.) separated by gender. This avoids unexpected litters of animals that you will have to care and find homes for.

Shopping

437. When you need an item shop for a used one instead of new in the classifieds, on Craigslist, at Goodwill and yard sales.

438. Put any desired purchase on a list along with the date you decided you wanted the item. If you still want the item in 30 days start shopping for it. This will help avoid impulse purchases.

439. Instead of buying an item check to see if something you already own will serve the purpose. For instance, empty jars can be reused as storage containers and shopping bags can have a second life as trash bags.

440. Instead of buying something see if you can make it instead. For instance, instead of eating out cook something at home. Instead of buying a funnel, make one using a plastic bottle.

441. Instead of buying expensive comforters use inexpensive sleeping bags instead. A cheap sleeping bag will work on a twin or full-size bed and be just as warm as the more expensive comforter.

442. Don't buy an item just because you have a coupon for it. The other choices available may still be cheaper.

443. Don't always buy the cheapest item. On some things it is better to pay a

little more. For instance, $10 shoes may last a week but $20 shoes could last a year or longer.

444. It is better to spend a few pennies more if you can walk to a store than it is to drive to another one. You will spend much more than those pennies in gasoline if you have to fire up your car.

445. Never buy when you can make do without.

446. If you know you will only use something once or twice, borrow or rent it instead of purchasing. This will save you money and eliminate the time you would otherwise have to care for it. If you purchase it the odds are that when you need it again you won't be able to locate it so why bother? Save your money instead.

447. Purely decorative items are a waste of money. Don't buy them.

448. Computers and other electronic items quickly become obsolete. Don't waste your money on the top-line stuff; aim for the lower-priced mid-grade items. They will be useful just as long and cost half as much or less.

449. Pieces from worn out leather belts can be used to make hinges on doors and boxes. Just nail the piece where the hinge would go. My grandfather's storage buildings all contained these hinges. Oil the leather occasionally with mineral oil, olive oil or neatsfoot oil to lengthen the life of the leather.

450. Place a leather or plastic flap over hasp locks to protect them from the weather and make them last longer without rusting.

451. A piece of board and a nail can replace the latch on a door or a gate[37]. Position

---

[37] http://www.howtodothings.com/home-garden/how-to-make-a-latch-for-a-wooden-fence-gate

the board where it will hold the door closed (it may have to be placed on the door or the frame depending on the swing of the door) and use a single nail in the center of the board. Turn the board to latch or release the door as desired.

452. Buying more than you can reasonably use is a waste. For instance, you can only use one set of sheets at a time on a bed so don't purchase more sheets if you already have 1-2 sheet sets per bed. It won't kill you to wash and replace them on the bed the same day. For accident-prone children keep two sets. Wash the dirty sheets immediately and keep them on hand to swap out for the next accident. The only exception to this rule would be if you don't own a washing machine and have to visit the laundromat. In that case, keep enough supplies on hand to last just long enough to make it to wash day.

453. If you feel you cannot live without a wall calendar pick one up at a local business for free. Some businesses put advertising at the bottom of the calendar. Clip these off with scissors to have it ad-free!

454. Ink pens are regularly given away at businesses, banks and doctor's offices. Stop in to say hi the next time your ink pen dies instead of buying one in a store.

455. Clean your hair brushes and combs by washing them with baking soda and warm water to increase their life span.

456. Stop collecting things. Collections can become expensive fast. Save that money instead by collecting free experiences with family and friends.

457. Make gifts for family and friends instead of buying them.

458. Shop clearance sales AFTER the holidays are over. You will save a fortune on candy and other holiday-related items.

459. Never shop on Black Friday despite the advertised deals. It isn't a bargain if you end up in the hospital after getting caught in the stampede of crazed shoppers or maced by a happy rent-a-cop. If you do hear of a good Black Friday deal, avoid the hazards of the crowds and buy it online.

460. Always verify that an advertised sales price is actually a sales price. Some stores will raise the price of an item for a couple of weeks, lower it back down to the everyday price and advertise it as a sale. Don't fall for it!

461. Ask for a rain check at a store if an advertised sales item is not available. I wonder if that would work at the car

dealer advertising incredibly low prices for "sold out" cars?

462. Avoid upgrading your stuff just because a new item is out. If what you have does what you need then keep it until it dies. This goes for computers, cars, phones, electronics and games.

463. When you are unhappy with the performance of an item you have recently purchased return it for a refund.

464. Use cash when shopping. You'll feel the bite more which will reduce how much you spend.

465. Only take as much cash as you are willing to spend on each trip. This eliminates overspending.

466. Leave your credit/debit/bank cards at home along with your checkbook. You can't buy things if your money is at home!

467. Avoid stores unless you absolutely need something. The less you visit the less you will spend.

468. Avoid extended warranties. Extended warranties are designed to run out just before the item actually decides to start breaking down, so save that money toward a new item when it finally wears out.

469. Make a list when you go shopping and don't allow yourself to deviate from the list. This will eliminate a fortune in impulse purchases.

470. When dealing with local merchants ask for a discount when you pay in cash. Remind them of the credit card fees you are saving them.

Travel

471. Bring food from home when you travel instead of eating out. Sandwiches are quick, cheap and easy.

472. Singles and couples can sleep in vehicles instead of renting expensive hotel rooms. Vans are especially convenient for this. Remove the back seats, add a kitty-litter commode and a mattress for comfort.

473. Consider couch-surfing or house swapping when you want to take a vacation.

474. Save up discount points and shop for off-season deals.

475. Go the scenic route to maximize the scenery and potential enjoyment of a journey. It may take a bit longer to get to your official destination but you may discover a memory that is more precious than the original destination ends up being.

476. Look for travel destinations close to home to reduce expenses. How many of you live in towns with tourist destinations that you have never visited? Check those out first for a local treat.

477. When traveling don't keep money in your pocket or purse. Stash it in your socks instead.

Utilities

478. Use curtains or doors to avoid heating and cooling rooms that you aren't using. Even a thin sheet draped over a doorway will shave money off your utility bill. Just make sure that any rooms with water pipes stay above freezing to protect the pipes from damage.

479. Close off rooms that you aren't going to be using for a period of time. For instance, shut the door to the kid's

rooms while they are at school. Heat the room back up to a comfortable temperature when they get home.

480. In the summer, cover the windows in your home that receive direct sunlight. Clip an emergency blanket to the window to reflect the sun's rays back outside. One lady shaved $70 off of her cooling bill with this one tip. You can find her story on The Simple Dollar[38] website.

481. In the winter hang blankets on outside walls to add extra insulation in these spots. Use large paper clamps and hang the clamps on small nails or push pins. This is similar to the old tradition of hanging tapestries in castles.

482. In the winter hang blankets over windows at night to add extra

---

[38] http://www.thesimpledollar.com/2010/06/30/energy-savings-with-a-solar-blanket-hair-clips-and-curtain-rods/

insulation to older windows. Remove during the day to allow the sunlight in.

483. During the winter hang blankets over outside doors to reduce any air seeping through the opening. This will help a lot, especially on doors that are unused.

484. Use Google Voice[39] to make and receive phone calls on your computer (requires high-speed Internet connection) for free. With a laptop this can replace your landline and your cell phone. Just make calls at the local Wi-Fi hot spots.

485. Use Google Voice for texting instead of a cell phone. Why pay when you can text for free?

486. If you have an iPad Touch, iPod or an Apple computer you can text, chat,

---

[39] http://www.google.com/voice

send photos or call your family and friends who own an iPhone (or other Apple device) using their built-in messaging system. FaceTime makes both video and regular phone calls while iMessage will send messages and photos among Apple devices.

487. Use Yahoo Messenger to text as well. This service is free as well but you will have to send the first text to users so that they can reply to communicate.

488. Use a MagicJack instead of a landline or cell phone. Some versions don't even require a computer when you're at home. It costs ~~$19.95~~ $29.95[40]/year for the original MagicJack which is hundreds of dollars less than traditional phone service. I use mine as a cell phone at local Internet hot spots. You can also connect it to computers at friend's houses to use

---

[40] They raised their rates in 2012.

your phone there as well. This is my phone service of choice.

489. If you have a friend who lives overseas that has access to high speed internet, send them an activated MagicJack so that you can talk to each other as much as you want for a lot less than it would cost otherwise. This would also allow your friend to call other people in the United States without those fees also, making this an excellent gift for overseas family members.

490. Use Yahoo Messenger, Google Talk and other instant messaging programs to voice and/or video chat with friends for free.

491. Skype enables users to call other users for free. You will need to pay if you want a regular telephone number or to call traditional phones though.

492. Use email instead of regular postal mail. Why buy a stamp when you can send an email for free?

493. Turn your thermostat down at night and keep warm under an extra blanket.

494. If you get cold at night snuggle down into a sleeping bag. The difference in warmth levels is incredible. On really cold nights toss an additional blanket over you to stay super toasty warm. Two sleeping bags combined work well to keep two people warm in the same area.

495. If you get cold at night wear socks and a hat. Heat loves to leave your body in these areas.

496. If your floors are very cold or damp in the winter make sure your bed is not in direct contact with the floor. While sleeping on the floor is nice and simple, a raised bed (or a frame for

your futon) will keep you much warmer on cold damp floors.

497. Pipe insulation can be repurposed into a door draft guard for less than it would cost for a commercial solution. You can find more information on Lifehacker[41].

498. Bubble wrap can be placed upon your windows for added insulation value.

499. Defrost refrigerators and freezers regularly to reduce the amount of energy they use. This does not apply to frost-free appliances, of course.

500. Manual Defrost refrigerators and freezers use less electricity than frost-free ones.

501. Place plastic bottles filled with water in your refrigerator and freezer to fill up some of the empty space. This will

---

[41] **http://lifehacker.com/5864865/repurpose-pipe-insulation-into-a-door-draft-guard?tag=repurpose**

save energy by helping your appliances work less to keep the area cool. They will also help to keep the items in your refrigerator and freezer cool during a power outage.

502. In the old days butter, milk and other items were submerged in wells and springs so that they would keep cold without refrigeration. If you live in the country you may want to try this.

503. If the power goes out in the winter you can save your refrigerated and frozen items by storing them outside. Just protect them from animals and let Mother Nature worry about the temps.

504. Place plastic on your windows (both inside and outside) to help lower heating and cooling bills. I use clear shipping tape to keep my plastic in place.

505. Save your water in the bathtub after bathing, You can use this water to hand-wash clothes and then recycle it a third time to water plants in the garden.

506. Catch the water in a container when you shower. Reuse the water to water plants, wash clothes and other purposes.

507. Take what is known as a Navy Shower by turning off the water when you lather and wash your hair then turn the water back on to rinse off to save water while bathing. They even have shower heads designed for this purpose now.

508. Turn the water off while scrubbing your hands to save additional money on your water bill.

509. If you heat with wood keep a chainsaw handy and offer to cut up and remove any fallen limbs in your

neighbor's yards. You can also drive out in the country after storms and remove limbs that have fallen across the road. This can provide a considerable amount of free firewood for wintertime.

510. Curtains hung about a canopy bed can help hold body heat in during the winter months, keeping the one sleeping within warmer so that the house thermostat can comfortably be lowered.

511. A gallon jug of frozen water will, when placed in front of a blowing fan, help to reduce the temperature in a hot room by circulating cooler air. The same effect can be had if the fan blows upon a damp towel.

512. Don't go in and out of your home very often in extremely hot or cold weather. Every time you open the doors you let out the warm/cold air so your home

has to use more energy to maintain a comfortable temperature.

513. Wear warm clothes in winter and turn the thermostat down. Save the shorts for summertime.

514. Unplug every electrical device when you are done using it. Most electric devices continue to draw small amounts of electricity even when they aren't in use so help your electric bill by pulling the plug. You can also connect them to a power strip and turn the whole strip off as well so save on your electric bill.

515. In the winter the Japanese will place a small heater under a low table and then cover that table with a thick cover that reaches to the floor. They place their legs under the cover to keep toasty without heating the whole room. Watch your heater placement to avoid a fire hazard.

516. Keep your feet warm in the winter by wearing wool socks. Wool stays warm even when the socks become damp from sweat or other moisture.

517. Keep your feet warm by changing your socks regularly. Sweaty feet will cause socks to get damp - and damp cotton socks will make your feet feel like icicles.

518. Avoid purchasing items that use electricity. For instance, standard wire telephones rely on electric produced by the telephone company while cordless telephones must have enough electric to power the base and keep the phone charged.

519. Use non-electric solutions whenever possible. For instance, use a spoon instead of an electric mixer, open the drapes instead of turning on a light, etc.

520. Soak your dried beans and rice to reduce the amount of time needed to cook them.

521. In the winter leave the oven door open when you are done using it. This allows the oven's remaining heat to filter into your living quarters for maximum benefit from the energy usage.

522. Use CFL or LED light bulbs instead of incandescent. These use significantly less energy than incandescent bulbs which will help to reduce your electric bill.

523. Reduce or eliminate your cell phone bill. If you have a MagicJack just take it with you and connect it to the computers of friends when you want to make a call or use it with free Wi-Fi if you own a laptop. Cellphones were virtually nonexistent before the 1990's and no one died from of lack of

communication. Remember that a cellphone is a luxury when you analyze the bill.

524. Assurance Wireless[42] offers free basic cell phone service for people who meet certain criteria. Visit their website to see if you qualify.

525. Slow down your Internet service. Unless you have 20 people using the same connection you should be fine using the lower speed tiers.

526. Split the Internet bill with a neighbor. Offer to share your Internet connection with a neighbor in exchange for half of the bill. Encrypt the connection and give them the password. If they don't pay one month, enter your router settings and block their computers. If you can get both of your neighbors to agree to

---

[42] http://www.assurancewireless.com/Public/Welcome.aspx

split the Internet bill (under the agreement that they can't tell anyone so they won't cause a stink) you could get your Internet for FREE.

527. If you live in an area where trash pickup is optional split the bill with a neighbor. Make sure that the both of you shred identifying trash (envelopes, letters, etc.) because some trash companies will dig through your bags for an excuse to charge you double.

528. Don't spend money to water your lawn. That is literally throwing money away for vanity. If it turns brown don't worry - it will come back when it rains.

529. Instead of wasting time and money raking, bagging and disposing fallen leaves every fall, leave them on the ground to provide fertilizer. Run over the leaves with a mower set on the

mulch setting if you want to help them compost quicker. Tree leaves are nature's grass fertilizer, yet so few people actually take advantage of it.

530. If you are going to be away from home for hours or days turn your water heater down (off is better) to save energy while you are gone.

531. Keep a washpan in your sink to catch the water you use when you wash your hands, brush your teeth, etc. Use this water to water your plants or flush your commode.

532. Turn the thermostat down on your water heater. This will reduce the amount of energy this appliance uses to keep your water warm.

533. If you ever have to replace your water heater go with an on-demand type. This way you won't have to spend money to keep the water warm

because it only heats the water you use as you use it.

534. Use the shortest vent hose possible when venting your dryer. Longer hoses trap more lint and are harder to clean, resulting in increased energy usage and fire risk.

535. Heat pumps can significantly reduce the cost of heating your home during the winter months.

536. Don't hang lights and decorations on the holidays. The extra electric usage can drastically increase your bill.

537. Plant deciduous trees around your home. The leaves will shade your home during the summer, making it easier to keep cool but fall off in the winter to allow you to take advantage of the sun in the cold months of winter.

538. Paint the roof of your mobile home white to better reflect the sun's rays and keep your home cooler. This works with any type of building that has a metal roof - not just mobile homes.

Conclusion

I must confess it has been a challenge dragging these tips from my muddled brain. I enjoyed the challenge however!

It is my hope that these tips not only help you but inspire you to come up with your own unique ways to save money and that you share your discoveries with others.

While the government keeps insisting that our economy is in the upswing I've a feeling that things are only going to get worse financially; the jobs we're accustomed to will pass and many in our world will struggle trying to earn a living in this changing world. Frugality and thrift will help us survive by reducing what we need to exist in the first place. This will make it easier to create an income to meet our needs.

Please help others learn of this book by leaving an honest review on the website of purchase. It is only by working together in this manner can we all help others survive this economic downturn.

Thank you,

Annie Jean Brewer

Appendix

To make your life easier I have included all of my personal articles that I simply referenced in the original ebook edition. In addition I am including some newer articles I have posted since this book was originally published that may help you in your pursuit of frugality as well.

Appendix Contents

How to Save Dried Nail Polish 180
How to Make Laundry Detergent at Home 182
How to Make a Single Gallon of Liquid Laundry Soap
 Detergent 188
How to Make Homemade Dishwashing Liquid 195
How to Make Homemade Liquid Soap 200
How to Clean Your Laundry on a Shoestring 205
Whiten Laundry Without Using Chlorine Bleach 212
How to Discreetly Save Money in the Bathroom 217
How to Make Tummy Tamer Candy with Ginger 224
How to Make Homemade Soy Milk 229
Pickle Juice for Dairy Intolerance 234
The Case of the Eggy Burps 237
Peanut Butter Puppy Cookies 240
How to Use Cloth in Animal Cages 244

How to Save Dried Nail Polish

This post was written by my daughter Katie. She is always thinking up frugal and crafty ideas so I persuaded her to share some of her tips with us.

Have you ever had your favorite fingernail polish dry up? Well I have and I was so sad when my favorite nail polish dried up so I got out the nail polish remover and poured some into my nail polish. After I did that I shook it up really well and just like magic it turned into a liquid.

It turned into a liquid because nail polish remover is made to remove hard nail polish and to do that it has to turn the dry nail polish into a liquid. If you have had your nail polish dry up try pouring nail polish remover in it. When you do that you will save your nail polish and have money left that can be used for something else so next time try saving your nail polish instead of tossing it in the trash.

How to Make Laundry Detergent at Home

Are you tired of paying high prices for laundry detergent, or simply want a more natural way to keep your family's clothes clean? You can make laundry detergent in the comfort of your own home for pennies a load, and no longer worry about allergies caused by unnecessary smells or chemicals.

First, decide whether you want to make liquid or powdered detergent. In my experience, the liquid detergent is a lot less expensive, but it takes more work and uses a lot of storage space. The powdered laundry detergent is simpler to make, takes up less space, but costs more per load to use. Weigh your options before you decide.

Second, gather up the supplies you will need to make your own laundry detergent at home. Here is a list:

Bar of soap. Most recommend Fels Naptha, Octagon, Zote or Ivory, but almost any bar soap will do. Fels Naptha is good for clothes that need a stronger detergent, while Ivory is great for its pureness. The only soap I do not recommend is Lever 2000. It has been reported to leave an odor in your clothing that is only apparent when the clothes get warm from wearing. If you use Fels Naptha or Zote, you will only need about 1/3 to ½ of a bar for a load. All other soaps will require at least a whole bar.

Borax. You will find this in the laundry section of most stores. The most common brand is 20 Mule Team. You will need ½ cup for these recipes.

Washing Soda (sodium carbonate). You used to be able to find this under the Arm & Hammer brand in most stores, but it is becoming almost impossible to find locally these days. However, in summer if you look in the pool supply section for pH raiser, you will be able to find this item listed under its chemical name sodium carbonate. Just check the ingredients listed on the containers of pH raiser in your local pool section to find this item. Do not confuse this with sodium bicarbonate, or baking soda, as baking soda has the opposite effect. Baking soda lowers the pH of the water, where sodium carbonate raises the pH of the water, making it more acidic and thus a better environment to clean your clothes. You will need ½ cup of this.

These three items are all you need to make basic laundry detergent, either liquid of powdered.

To make powdered detergent, grate the soap as small as you can. If you leave the bar unwrapped for a while before grating it will grate much finer than if you grate it straight from the wrapper. Some people use food processors for this step, while I have learned that my blender does this acceptably well in small batches. Grate the soap as fine as you can; you can use a hand grater if you want and then rub the shavings between your hands to break them up even more, so there is no need to purchase any equipment for this step.

After the soap is grated mix well with the borax and washing soda, adding ½ cup of oxy-clean if you desire, and you are finished! Store in a covered container and use one tablespoon on smaller or lightly soiled loads, or two tablespoons for heavier soiled items!

This does not lather much if any, so it is safe to use even in he- laundry machines, and has been used by numerous people without any issues.

To make liquid detergent takes a bit more work. Take the grated soap and mix it into a couple of quarts of water in a large pan. Place on low heat and stir until the all the soap is dissolved, then add the borax and washing soda. Do NOT add Oxy-clean to the liquid detergent recipe! It will foam and render the batch unusable.

Stir until the contents are well mixed, then remove from heat. Place a gallon of cool water into a five gallon bucket, and then pour your soap mixture in, mixing well. Add enough water to finish filling the bucket, stirring well, then cover and let sit overnight. This will look like goop, but it will clean your clothes! You need ½ cup of this mixture per load of clothes. Store some in a repurposed liquid laundry or fabric softener container to make it easier to use.

This makes five gallons of liquid laundry detergent.

When most think of making homemade laundry they think the process will be expensive and complicated, but the opposite is true. It is very easy to make your own laundry detergent at home for not only less than the store bought varieties cost, but without all of those unwanted chemicals.

How to Make a Single Gallon of Liquid Laundry Soap Detergent

There are a lot of recipes floating around the Internet with instructions to make both liquid and powdered laundry soap at home; most use similar ingredients but leave out a few key facts:

Liquid laundry soap is MUCH less expensive to make than powdered. A good batch of liquid laundry soap can cost as much as the powdered version but since the ingredients are already dissolved and mixed it takes less to clean the same amount of clothes.

Liquid laundry soap cleans better in cold water because the soap flakes are already dissolved; powdered laundry soap still contains the grated soap flakes which must first dissolve before working (and those flakes dissolve better in warm water).

The majority of liquid laundry soap recipes are designed to make a huge batch of cleaner and for the average family those 5 to 10 gallon batches of laundry soap are not only unwieldy but require large buckets and containers that are difficult to acquire and difficult to store as well. Simply trying to use basic math to cut the recipes down can be a nightmare in logistics: how do you reasonably cut down a recipe for 10 gallons of laundry soap when it only takes 1/2 bar of Fels Naptha- it seems as if that tiny amount is insufficient to clean ANYTHING, much less your dirty clothes!

After much thought and consideration I have managed to successfully create a recipe for a single gallon of liquid laundry soap. This recipe takes a minimum of ingredients, works up in minutes, cleans just as well and stores a LOT easier than those five gallon buckets we've stashed in the days of yore. It is also much more frugal than the powdered version and works better in cold water as the soap is already dissolved.

Things You'll Need:
1 cup grated Fels Naptha or Zote Soap
1/3 cup Borax
1/3 cup Washing Soda (Sodium Carbonate)
1 Gallon of Water
Empty 1.5 gallon container (recommended, but a 1-gallon container will work)
2 quart saucepan
Long-handled spoon
Funnel
Hot Plate or stovetop burner

Step One:
Pour 1 quart of water into the saucepan.

Step Two:
Turn the stovetop burner temperature onto medium.

Step Three:
Add the grated Fels Naptha or Zote soap to the water.

Step Four:
Stir the soap mixture with the spoon over medium heat until the soap is completely dissolved.

Step Five:
Add the Borax and the Washing Soda to the dissolved soap in the saucepan.

Step Six:
Stir the mixture for a few minutes until the ingredients are thoroughly mixed and the solution thickens into a syrupy consistency. Do not allow the mixture to boil; if needed,

reduce the stovetop temperature to maintain a slow simmer.

Step Seven:
Pour the remaining water into the 1.5 gallon container (if using a 1 gallon container only pour about half of the water in at this time).

Step Eight:
Pour the dissolved soap solution into the container using the funnel to avoid spills.

Step Nine:
Tightly cap the container and shake well to thoroughly mix the contents. If using a 1 gallon container, add the remaining water to the container, but leave an inch of space for shaking the solution before use.

How to Use:
Add 3/4 to 1 cup of the liquid laundry soap to a load of laundry depending upon how dirty the fabric is. Smaller washers may need to reduce the soap down to 1/2 cup for light cleaning jobs.

This is a low-sudsing but effective cleaner.

Tips:

To boost the cleaning power of this liquid laundry soap (or any laundry cleaner) add 1/2 to 1 cup of Ammonia to the wash water as you add the clothes. The ammonia will help cut grease and stains better, adds a slight disinfection capability to the wash and will not cause your laundry to smell like ammonia. Ammonia has also been used to whiten whites instead of bleach and in my experiments is quite effective at doing so.

If you cannot locate Washing Soda in your area, go to the pool supply section of your local hardware store and look for pH raiser. Read the ingredients of the pH raisers to locate one made with Sodium Carbonate. This is the exact same thing that Washing Soda is made of, so you can substitute this in the place of washing soda. Baking Soda is NOT the same; it is designed to neutralize pH while washing soda raises the pH of the water so do not attempt to substitute baking soda for washing soda in your liquid laundry soap.

You can acquire a 1.5 gallon container to hold your liquid laundry soap by recycling a large bleach container–the largest ones at the store are rated to hold slightly under the 1.5 gallon amount but work perfectly for this purpose.

How to Make Homemade Dishwashing Liquid

Dishwashing liquid is a necessity in the average household but store-bought brands may contain unwanted chemicals or simply be too expensive for the budget.

With a few supplies you can make your own dishwashing liquid at home for pennies a gallon that will not only clean just as well as the expensive brands but will be better on the environment as well.

Things You'll Need:
1.5 gallon container (1 gallon will work but larger is preferred).
1/2 bar Zote Soap (1/4 of a large bar)
1 gallon of water
1 Tbsp Washing Soda
Wooden Spoon
2 quart saucepan
Funnel

Step One:
Grate the 1/2 bar of Zote soap.

Step Two:
Place 1 quart of water into the sauce pan and heat on medium until warm.

Step Three:
Turn the heat down to medium low and pour the grated Zote soap into the water.

Step Four:
Stir the Zote soap mixture until the flakes are completely dissolved. Turn your heat down if it starts to boil.

Step Five:

Add the tablespoon of washing soda to the melted Zote soap mixture.

Step Six:

Stir for several minutes until the mixture thickens. It will resemble a thin syrup when done.

Step Seven:

Pour the remaining water into your 1.5 gallon container. If you are using a 1-gallon container, pour 1/2 gallon into the container instead to allow shaking room.

Step Eight:

Pour the Zote soap mixture into the 1.5 gallon container.

Step Nine:

Cap the container tightly and shake the contents thoroughly.

Step Ten:

If using a 1-gallon container, uncap and fill

with the remaining water, leaving 1-inch of headspace for shaking.

Step Eleven:
Allow the mixture to cure overnight.

Step Twelve:
Shake well and use in the place of your regular dishwashing liquid. Note that this does not lather as much as regular dishwashing liquid because it has no special chemicals to create unnecessary foam.

Tips:
Washing soda is normally found in the laundry section of your grocery store, but you can use certain types of pH raisers from the pool supply section if necessary. For more information on washing soda, including a link where to purchase it at a reasonable price online you can visit my blog post on the subject. Please note that baking soda is NOT the same as washing

soda and cannot be substituted successfully in this recipe.

Zote Soap is a soap commonly used in the Hispanic community for washing dishes and cleaning laundry. It can be found online and at various grocers; some smaller stores will order it in if you request it. Check out the book *"The Minimalist Cleaning Method"* for more tips and recipes using Zote Soap.

I used to recommend Octagon soap instead of Zote but it is no longer being manufactured.

Zote Soap can be found at grocers for a price of less than a dollar a bar; the store where I purchase sells it for 79 cents. At this price, a gallon of homemade dishwashing liquid costs approximately 40 cents a gallon.

How to Make Homemade Liquid Soap

Walk into the soap section of your local store and brace yourself. The price of everything-including liquid soap-is going up. To make your money go farther you can make your own liquid soap for pennies instead of shelling out several dollars at the store. With a minimum of ingredients you can make your next batch of liquid soap in minutes, saving money and helping the environment by reducing the amount of plastic bottles you send to the landfill. You can even get the kids in on the act by having them grate the soap for you-teaching them how to conserve money in the process.

Ingredients:
1/2 bar of soap (Ivory recommended, but any brand of bar soap will do)
1 quart of water
1 quart of water
2 quarts of water

Tools needed:
1 pan, 2 quart size
Stirring spoon or whisk
Grater
1 re-purposed gallon container with lid (1.5 gallon recommended for extra shaking room)
Empty pump soap dispenser

Step 1:
Grate the bar of soap. The finer you grate the soap the faster and easier it will melt.

Step 2:

Place the grated soap in a pan with a quart of water.

Step 3:

Heat the grated soap and water on medium heat, stirring until all the soap is completely melted.

Step 4:

Pour one quart of cool water into a re-purposed gallon container while the soap is melting.

Step 5:

Pour the melted soap mixture into the gallon container containing the quart of cool water. Cap and shake well to mix.

Step 6:

Pour as much of the remaining water into the gallon container as will fit. If you used a 1.5 gallon container, fill it to the 1 gallon mark.

Step 7:

Cap the container and let it sit overnight to cure.

Step 8:

To use, shake the container and then fill your empty liquid soap dispenser. Use just like you would traditional liquid soap.

This recipe makes 1 gallon of liquid soap.

The cost of this soap will vary depending upon the brand of soap that you use. To compare the cost with commercially available liquid soap: If the bar of soap cost fifty cents (common price in 2011 per bar in a multi-pack of soap), you can create 2 gallons of liquid soap from a single $0.50 bar. This is a significant savings when compared to what a liquid soap refill costs to purchase!

If you use bar soap, you can save the slivers until you get the equivalent of a half of a bar and use that instead of buying a bar of soap.

Add a few drops of olive oil to the mixture for a natural moisturizing effect.

How to Clean Your Laundry on a Shoestring

Laundry expenses can quickly eat a chunk out of the average family budget. Detergents, spot treaters, whiteners and fabric softeners are not only expensive but may contain unwanted chemicals as well.

The fabric care industry doesn't want you to know that you can keep your laundry clean for a LOT less than you expect. Here are a few tips to keep those clothes looking new for longer:

Don't Wash Unless It's Needed:

If you wore something for a short time and it does not have any obvious dirt or stains, hang it up and allow it to air out instead of tossing it in the wash. This will reduce the wear on the garment from washing as well as reduce the amount of water, electricity and chemicals you need to keep it looking its finest. You can wear some items several times before washing them and reduce your cleaning bill even more.

Pre-Treat (but not with the Advertised Stuff):

Grab a bar of Octagon or Fels Naptha soap and dip one end into some water to moisten. Rub upon the spots, moistening the bar as needed to work the soap into the fabric. Rub the spot well to work the soap in and wash at a later time (allow to sit on the spot for several minutes at the least).

Separate Your Laundry:

Separating your whites from colors is one of the most important things you can do when cleaning your laundry. This allows the whites to remain free of the dyes that leach off of the other clothes, enabling them to stay a brighter white. If you have a large number of a certain color or type of clothing (like jeans), washing them separately can keep them looking their finest. The more you can reasonably sort your laundry into colors, the better your laundry will turn out-but don't go overboard. It is perfectly okay to just sort into whites and coloreds, or whites, lights and darks.

Use Homemade Laundry Soaps:

Commercial laundry detergents are not only expensive but contain chemicals that may irritate your skin. Homemade laundry soaps are made with very few ingredients and can be worked up quickly at a cost of approximately 75 cents a gallon. These cleaners, including a powdered version, only contain what you want them to contain and eliminate the heavy perfumes that can bother your sinuses.

Boost Your Laundry Detergent With Ammonia:

Ammonia is an inexpensive cleaner that removes body oils and other greasy dirt from laundry with ease. Add 1/2 cup per load of laundry can brighten and freshen your wardrobe in a surprising manner by removing the buildup your laundry detergents and fabric softeners leave behind. Ammonia is also excellent at whitening dull whites–just don't add it if you are using bleach! Instead use ammonia as your everyday whitener, and rotate with bleach on your whites for an occasional boost to minimize the fabric deterioration that bleach can cause. Don't worry–your clothes will not have an ammonia smell after using this laundry booster!

The Extra Rinse:

Modern top-load washing machines only allow for a single rinse which can leave soap residues behind on your laundry. These residues will attract dirt to your clothes faster, making them look dirty sooner. An extra rinse will remove that extra residue, allowing your clothes to be as clean as possible for as long as possible.

Use Vinegar:

Vinegar is an acid that will help your washer to remove the last vestiges of soap from your clean laundry. When combined with an extra rinse it enables your clothes to get extra clean. A gallon of vinegar costs less than $3 in most areas–a lot less than bottles of fabric softener a portion of the size! Use 1/2 cup per load in the final rinse by placing in the fabric softener dispenser or using a softener ball to dispense the liquid when needed. Vinegar also has another added benefit in washers with fabric softener dispensers–it won't clog up your dispenser in the slightest!

Remove Promptly From The Dryer:

Removing your laundry from the dryer in a prompt manner will help to prevent wrinkles from setting in your clean clothes, reducing the amount you need to iron. If you are unable to remove your clothes promptly you can toss a damp cloth into your dryer and allow to run for a few minutes to remove some of the wrinkles. If this is a recurring issue, you may want to consider hanging your damp clothes on hangers and allowing them to dry naturally instead of using the dryer to avoid the wrinkle issue.

These tips will enable you to have a beautifully clean wash at a fraction of the price, creating breathing room in your budget while giving you cleaner clothes at the same time.

Whiten Laundry Without Using Chlorine Bleach

Whites-they are beautiful when new but can quickly become dingy over time. Chlorine bleach is a harsh way to whiten laundry, shortening fabric life and leaving a yellowish hue caused by oxidation. Color-safe bleaches are often ineffective, leaving most users frustrated and avoiding white items in future purchases.

There is a little-known secret to whitening laundry that does not require bleach, a secret weapon that you may have under your kitchen sink right now. That secret is ammonia. Ammonia is a heavy-duty cleaning and degreasing agent, capable of removing stains that other cleaners can't. The primary thing about using ammonia is to avoid all contact with bleach. Depending upon the concentration of each substance, bleach and ammonia can produce a deadly gas or even explode under the right conditions, so be cautious and avoid mixing the two substances.

Things You'll Need:

- Dirty load of whites
- Top-load washing machine
- 1 cup of ammonia
- 1/4 teaspoon of Mrs. Stewart's Laundry Blueing (for an extra-bright white)
- 1/2 cup vinegar or fabric softener for the rinse (vinegar recommended)

Step One:
Fill the washing machine with hot water.

Step Two:
Add the recommended amount of your preferred laundry detergent to the washer.

Step Three:
Add 1 cup of ammonia to the washer.

Step Four:
Add 1/4 teaspoon of Mrs. Stewart's laundry blueing to the washer. Note: washer water should be a light blue tint after adding this.

Step Five:
Allow the washer to agitate for a moment to mix these items thoroughly.

Step Six:
Add your whites to the washer. Make sure that the laundry has plenty of room to agitate (do not overstuff the washer).

Step Seven:
Allow your washer to thoroughly agitate your laundry on a long cycle. If your washer does not have two rinse cycles, turn

your knob back during the rinse cycle to give your clothes that second rinse cycle. This extra rinse helps to make sure your washer removes as much leftover detergent from your laundry as possible, which will lessen discoloration of your whites.

Step Eight:
Add the fabric softener or vinegar to the final rinse cycle.

Step Nine:
Dry your laundry as usual.

Using ammonia instead of bleach on your white laundry will eliminate the yellowing that is common in bleached items. It will also reduce or eliminate any stains already on the white laundry, causing it to be whiter. Mrs. Stewart's Laundry Blueing is an optical brightener that has been in use for generations and will give your whites that "pop" so loved on new white items. Using vinegar instead of fabric softener will help your washer remove any detergent residue left on the laundry without leaving an overpowering smell.

Sources:

http://www.tiphero.com/tips_754_whitening-clothes-cutting-detergent-use.html

http://quolkids.com/information/earthcare/articles/friendly_cleaning_products.htm

http://ths.gardenweb.com/forums/load/laundry/msg1220470723573.html

http://www.wisegeek.com/what-is-ammonia.htm

How to Discreetly Save Money in the Bathroom

Family Cloths are a very private way to save money at home. By using cloth to wipe your private areas after using the bathroom you are not only saving money by not using bathroom tissue but you are helping the environment in a small way by eliminating a disposable product from your life.

Four Hesitations About Using Family Cloths

The first hesitation some have is the instant ick factor associated with using cloth and washing it as opposed to using disposable paper. There is not much difference in washing family cloths than dirty underwear-both contain bodily solids and fluids.

The second hesitation is a concern over cleanliness. When wiping with cloth as opposed to paper you are free to use an extra cloth or so if you feel "less than fresh"-just toss it in the wash and you can reuse it. Compare this to regular bathroom tissue-how many children get scolded and conditioned to use less tissue to save money in the family budget? Have you seen the underwear of children conditioned to conserve bathroom tissue? It's not a pretty sight. With family cloths you can encourage your family members to use what is needed to get clean, and even provide a bottle of liquid to help them with the chore!

The third hesitation is the gross-out factor of washing the cloths, but using the proper method you will not have to touch the soiled cloths.

The fourth hesitation is summed up as "What will the neighbors [family, friends] think?" Properly executed, no one will notice that you are using family cloths unless you actually tell them.

How to Begin Using Family Cloths
To actually begin using family cloths very little is needed.

The supply list:

Washcloths
Covered bucket or pail
Water
1/4 bleach or vinegar
Squirt of soap

Step One - Preparing the Family Cloth Bucket

Prepare your bucket by filling half full of water and adding 1/4 bleach or vinegar and a splash of soap. Soaking the cloths in this solution will reduce odors and germs as well as allowing the cloths to come cleaner in the wash. If you do not have bleach or vinegar add some borax to the water instead, but bleach is the preferred liquid for it's germ-killing properties. If your bucket is small or large you may want to increase or decrease the amount used. A half ounce of bleach per gallon of water makes a very weak sanitizer solution that is used to clean food preparation surfaces in restaurants. Do not use too much bleach- this will damage your cloths.

Place this bucket in an inconspicuous place within reach of your commode. I use a re-purposed laundry detergent bucket placed between the commode and vanity- my washer and dryer are in my bathroom, so no one notices a container of laundry detergent nearby! This is where you will store the used cloths until washday.

Step Two - Placing the Family Cloths

Place a pile or basket of washcloths within reach of the commode. The reason washcloths are chosen over other fabrics like re-purposed tee-shirts or flannel is simple: camouflage. No one thinks twice about a pile of washcloths in a bathroom, so you can hide these in plain view! Extra cloths can be purchased inexpensively at places like Wal-Mart-in January of 2010 the Southside Paducah Wal-Mart was selling an 18-pack of washcloths in white or a color assortment for $4.

Make sure you keep a roll of bathroom tissue in plain view at all times-this will make you look like you are using bathroom tissue the same as "everyone else."

Step Three - Using the Family Cloths

When you use the restroom grab a washcloth and use it to wipe instead. If you want to get really clean take a re-purposed squirt bottle (a dishwashing liquid or shampoo bottle is perfect) and fill with water and add a couple drops of tea tree oil (antiseptic), a couple drops or olive or mineral oil (skin conditioning - you can even use hair conditioner or lotion here), and a couple drops of liquid soap. Squirt this liquid on your cloth before wiping your private areas to get really clean.

When you are finished wiping place the cloth in the covered bucket, flush the commode and wash your hands.

Step Four - Washing the Family Cloths

Take the bucket and pour it into your washer. Spin the water out of the cloths and wash them in hot water with bleach. Use vinegar instead of fabric softener in the rinse to get them extra clean. Dry well and place the cloths back in use!

Notes about using Family Cloths

Do not use a trash can to store your family cloths in. Someone will invariably toss a nasty piece of trash in there for you to fish out. Marking it as "Do Not Use" will only raise questions from company. Concealment is key. You can place your bucket in a covered wicker basket, or even stash it in the bottom of a laundry hamper- just do not use a trash can or diaper pail unless you are prepared for discovery.

Now go out and save some money!

How to Make Tummy Tamer Candy with Ginger

An upset tummy is torture to a child. When they can't keep anything down it is even worse. A natural remedy for upset stomach is ginger but getting spicy ginger into the body of an ill child can be a challenge. Enter Tummy Tamer Candy. Children love candy and rarely pass up the opportunity to make Mom and Dad happy by keeping some in their mouth. This recipe not only incorporates the beneficial properties of ginger but chamomile as well to soothe your child and send him on the road to recovery.

Ingredients:
2 cups sugar
1-1/4 cups brewed Sweet Dreams tea (or regular chamomile tea)
1 Tbsp. powdered ginger

Mix all of the ingredients in a heavy pot over medium heat and allow to boil until you reach the soft-crack phase. Stir constantly while boiling to keep from sticking. To determine soft crack phase, put a spoonful in a cup of cold water-soft crack strands will hold together while still being somewhat soft. If you overcook do not worry-it will still turn out but just be a bit harder to work with.

When it is ready pour it onto a well-buttered baking sheet. Any type of flexible metal pan will do, I personally use an aluminum pizza pan. Spread the mixture into a thin layer and let cool until it hardens.

After it hardens break it up into pieces and ask your child to suck on as many pieces of the candy as they wish.

Tips:

Any type of beneficial tea will work. I have used echinacea tea in this recipe as well.

You may have to adjust the ginger level up or down depending upon your child's tolerance for spicy flavors.

The ginger used in this recipe is standard ginger found in the spice section of the grocery store. You can grind fresh ginger to make this or make a ginger tea and eliminate the powdered spice but in my experience fresh ginger is too tangy for a young child and they refuse the candy.

When brewing the tea, give it a longer than normal steep time or use two tea bags to give it a rich concentration of beneficial herbs. You may even want to try two different types of tea bags at once like a bag of echinacea and a bag of chamomile brewing in the hot water simultaneously.

Warnings:

Verify that your child does not have an allergy to chamomile (or whatever ingredient you choose for the tea) before adding to the recipe. If the child does have an allergy substitute water.

Note:

This recipe is an original creation. It was created out of desperation one weekend several years ago when my daughter was unable to hold anything down including standard anti-nausea formulas. I asked her to keep a piece of the candy in her mouth and slowly her stomach calmed. Being a preschooler she was delighted to do such a pleasant "favor" for mommy! Since then I keep a batch on hand for whenever any of us has an upset stomach, and my daughter gave it the name so she could request it if we ran out.

How to Make Homemade Soy Milk

Soymilk is a blessing for those allergic to cow's milk or on vegetarian diets. The price of it, however, takes a bite out of our wallets with a half-gallon costing over $3 in most areas of the country in 2011. You can make soymilk at home with a few simple tools for significant savings. A pound of organic soybeans can make a whole gallon of soymilk for less cost than a gallon of cow's milk–making it more economical to switch.

A second benefit of making soymilk at home is the fact that you will know exactly what your soymilk contains–there will be nothing it unless you put it there.

A third benefit is the ability to always have fresh soymilk by making it up in quantities perfect for your family. By keeping soybeans in the pantry you won't have to run to the grocery to buy milk–just make some more!

A fourth benefit is the ability to use the whole bean if you desire. You can use the beans left over from the milk extraction process in breads and other foods like Tempeh if you desire!

Note: This makes 1 quart of fresh soymilk.

Things You'll Need:
4 ounces of soybeans
Quart container with lid
2 quarts of water
Blender

2 quart saucepan
Spoon
Loosely woven cloth like cheesecloth
Strainer
Salt, sugar and/or vanilla to taste

Step One:

Place the 4 ounces of soybeans in one quart of water and allow to soak overnight. If in a hurry you can heat to boiling for a couple of minutes then allow to sit for an hour or so for a fast soak. Note that this will change the flavor of the soymilk slightly.

Step Two:

Drain the soaked soybeans and place in a blender with a quart of water.

Step Three:

Process the soybeans on high for 45 seconds or until the beans are thoroughly chopped. The liquid will turn milky.

Step Four:

Place the strainer over the saucepan and lay the cheesecloth in the strainer leaving the edges out where they can be easily grabbed.

Step Five:

Pour the blended soybeans into the cheesecloth-lined strainer.

Step Six:

Grab the edges of the cheesecloth and twist together. The beans will form a solid ball within the cheesecloth.

Step Seven:

Squeeze the remaining liquid out of the soybeans. The remaining soybean is called "okara" and can be used in cooking or making Tempeh if desired.

Step Eight:

Boil the soymilk for ten minutes, stirring constantly to avoid boiling over.

Step Nine:

Pour the soymilk into the quart container. Flavor the soymilk with a pinch of salt, a teaspoon of vanilla and/or a teaspoon of sugar if desired.

Step Ten:

Store the soymilk in the refrigerator and use within a few days.

Tips:

If you don't have a scale to weigh out four ounces of soybeans just portion out 1/4 of a pound of soybeans.

Double the recipe to make a half gallon of soymilk. You may have to process the beans in two batches depending upon the size of your blender.

Source:

Soya: How to Make Soymilk[43]

---

[43] **http://www.soya.be/how-to-make-soy-milk.php**

Pickle Juice for Dairy Intolerance

Growing up in a home that loved dairy, it broke my heart when I discovered that my system no longer tolerated the cheeses, ice creams and milk that I craved. My doctor said I had two choices: I could avoid all things dairy or I could simply live with the unpleasant results of my indulgence.

I have discovered another solution.

It was a coincidence the first time I drank pickle juice with dairy products. We were having cheeseburgers for dinner and had used up the last pickles in the jar. I drank the dregs of the juice before tossing the container and to my surprise I didn't have to visit the restroom immediately after dinner!

Since then I have started eating pickles and drinking the juice whenever I partake of dairy products. As a result, I no longer have any stomach issues from my indulgence. I eat a lot of pickles these days but who cares if it works?

I have only tried this with dill pickles so I have no clue if it will work for other pickle varieties. The only thing I can say with any certainty is that dill pickles and their juice have made a remarkable difference in my level of dairy tolerance, so hopefully it will work for you as well.

This does nothing for any sinus issues caused by dairy – I have to use an over the counter allergy med for that – but the stomach problems were by far the worst of my two symptoms so I am definitely not complaining.

The Case of the Eggy Burps

These past few days have been a bit of a migraine haze. I've done little more than lay on the couch praying that the world would just. Leave. Me. Alone.

When the pain finally subsided I found myself beset with a case of those nasty eggy burps – the ones that smell and taste like rotten eggs. Ugh.

I Googled and dug through my home remedies. Not a single home remedy referenced this icky tasting malady and most references to it online declared I was afflicted with a horrible parasite "GO TO THE DOCTOR NOW" sorta thing.

I knew I didn't have a parasite; something was out of balance in my system, probably from that darned migraine. Parasites can't handle the copious amounts of pickles and pickle juice I ingest.

I spread out my research net and discovered a simple recipe for indigestion: 1 teaspoon of baking soda dissolved in a cup of water, drank slowly.

I mixed it up and sipped. The taste reminded me of Alka-Seltzer but without the fizz. It wasn't unpleasant at all. Within a few minutes I burped twice – actual, normal-tasting burps. Next my system released one final eggy burp —

And all was at peace in my stomach.

No more roiling. No more bubbling. No more constant belching and gas-passing. It had ended as abruptly as it begun, all thanks to water and baking soda.

So if you ever find yourself beset with the eggy burps, also known as sulphur burps, mix a teaspoon of baking soda in a cup of water and drink it down. It worked for me.

Peanut Butter Puppy Cookies

We love our pets and the dog treat industry knows it. Walk down the treat aisle at your local pet store and you will discover not only an incredible variety for your pets but an astounding price point as well. In this economy most of us cannot afford $5-$10 or more for a simple treat to give Fido and fortunately we don't have to. With a few supplies and an oven we can whip up a simple doggie treat that we can not only create to size for our extremely tiny or large pets but that fits our budget a LOT better than current pet treat prices. As an added advantage you will know exactly what these cookies contain as well as what they don't–no added sugar, no artificial colors or flavors–just simple goodness at a cost of a few pennies and a little time.

Things You Need:

- Mixing bowl
- Spoon
- Baking sheets
- Knife or cookie cutter
- 2 Cups Wheat Flour (or 1 cup all-purpose and 1 cup whole wheat flour)
- 1 Cup Quick Cook Oats (can use old fashioned oats but avoid instant)
- 1/3 Cup Peanut Butter (Whatever you have, chunky or smooth it does not matter)
- 1-1/4 cups warm water (steam rising from water)

Note: Preheat oven to 350 degrees Fahrenheit.

Step One:
Place flour and oats in the bowl and mix.

Step Two:
Add Peanut butter and water.

Step Three:
Stir until well mixed. All the flour should be scraped off of the sides of the bowl. Add a little more flour if the dough is sticky.

Step Four:
Place dough on a well-floured surface and knead for one minute, adding flour as needed to keep the dough from sticking to your hands.

Step Five:
Roll or pat out dough to 1/4-inch thickness. A uniform thickness is important for even baking.

Step Six:
Cut the dough into pieces using a knife of a cookie cutter. For little dogs use a knife to cut a 1-inch grid for treats just right for those pocket-sized pets. For larger dogs you can make a grid of 2-inch squares for a small bite or go even larger depending upon the dog and your preference.

Step Seven:
Place treats 1-inch apart on baking sheets and place in preheated oven.

Step Eight:
Bake treats for 20 minutes.

Step Nine:
Allow to cool well before serving.

Tips:
These treats keep really well in the refrigerator or freezer but can be stored on a shelf if kept extremely dry. To ensure sufficient dryness for long-term storage you can place overnight in a dehydrator.
Every oven bakes differently so you may have to cook these for shorter or longer times. The treats will be golden brown when done.

How to Use Cloth in Animal Cages

This was originally posted on my blog in 2010.

Those who have been following me for a while know that I probably indulge my kid a bit too much when it comes to pets. She has puppies, fish, birds and guinea pigs–and mom gets stuck taking care of all of them!

The guinea pigs are by far the messiest and smelliest of the bunch to care for. If you use wood chips they throw them everywhere, they are a pain to change and start stinking pretty quick. Besides that, the cost of wood chips (or carefresh, recycled paper or whatever else you use) adds up quick!

Earlier this summer I started having a problem with flies. When changing the wood chips didn't work, I decided to use cloth in the bottom of his cage and change it daily to eliminate their nesting ground. That actually worked. It not only worked, but ended up being easier to care for than using the darn wood chips!

Now that the flies are under control I no longer change the cage daily, but instead change it on the days that I wash my family cloths. On those days I remove the guinea pig and his stuff, take the top off of the cage and grab the top cloth (a solid piece of muslin currently) by the four corners to catch his poo mess. This top cloth is carried outside to a grown up section of yard and shaken out really well to get rid of the mess.

The remaining cloths as well as the top cloth are then placed in my washer with the family cloths, spun out and given a good washing and sanitizing before being hung out to dry.

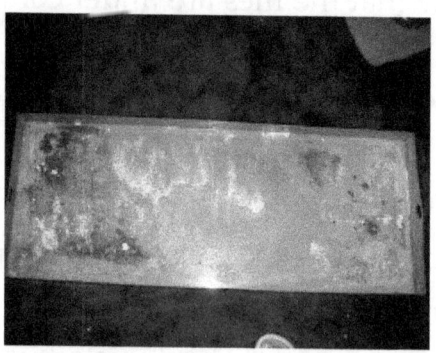

This is the empty cage bottom. The white is a thin layer of baking soda for odor control and the brown is rust spots (it's an old cage).

Upon this empty bottom I start layering my towels.

They are smaller terrycloth towels I purchased in bulk from Sam's Club and three of them covers the bottom with a bit of overlap. I keep layering them until they are about an inch thick, placing extra padding on the ends where he tends to lay and urinate:

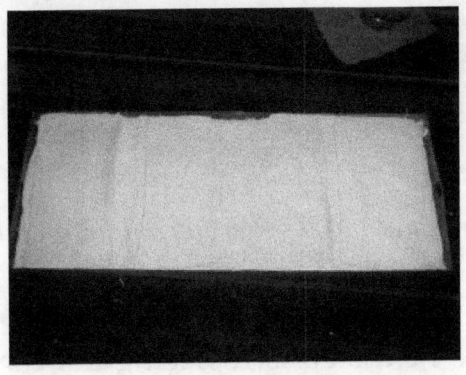

As you can see the layers come to the top of the cage tray. Then I take a piece of muslin with some overlap and lay it over this absorbent layer. This serves two purposes: it keeps the guinea pig from nibbling on the terrycloth or becoming caught in the loops, and creates a side guard to protect your furniture and floor. It also gives you something clean to grab onto when you go to change the cage!

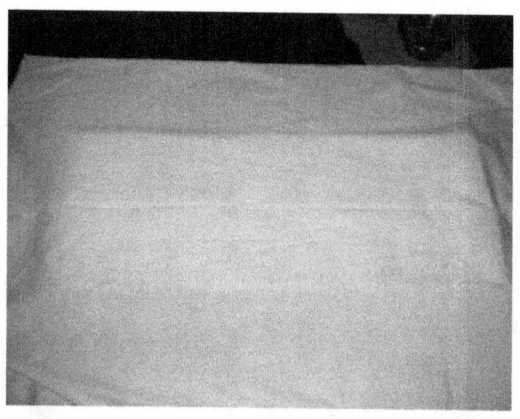

The muslin has a generous border on all four sides of the cage bottom

The next step is replacing the cage top, and securing it to the bottom through the muslin.

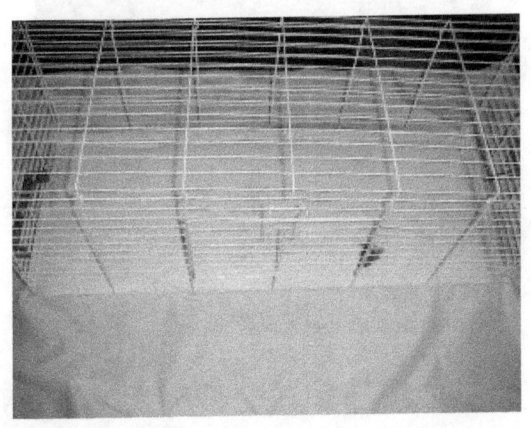

Latch the cage top to the bottom and leave the muslin margins free.

After the cage top is secured, secure the fabric margins to the side of the cage using safety pins. I generally leave the cage door open during this part to make sure I leave enough slack to easily open and close the cage door.

Replace the animal's food and toys, and you are finished!

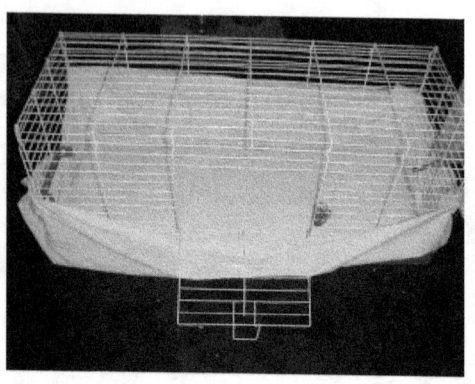

Leave enough slack to enable easy opening of the cage door.

Voila! You now have a cage liner that is no-sew and entirely reusable! It is also quicker to change using the fabric than it ever was when I used wood chips!

Some prefer using a layer of polar fleece with the argument that it keeps the animal dryer. If I had some I would try it but for now muslin will have to do because that is what I have on hand. I was going to purchase enough at Wal Mart the other day to make two liner sheets but there was a long line at the fabric counter and no employee in sight so I decided to continue using the muslin for right now. Why buy something new when what I have works well enough already?

Bugsy tends to go poo on the edges so he doesn't walk in his mess any more than if he were on wood chips. I also wash whites every few days (slightly more than once a week) so he gets changed more often than when he was on the wood chips.

He seems to like this more and I like the fact that I am reusing something instead of killing a tree or wasting paper every time I clean his cage.

This may be an option for you to consider if you want to reduce how much you spend and perhaps benefit the environment. I've gotten some cloths here that have been in service since 1997 and are still going strong (even if they are a bit shaggy). That is a lot of use from one item when you compare that to something like wood chips or paper that gets purchased, used and then immediately discarded.

I know my house smells better from the more regular cleaning, and the guinea pig seems happier! I am happier that his cage is easier to clean and I no longer have to purchase wood chips for the bottom of it!

About the Author

Annie Jean Brewer has been writing since she was old enough to put pencil to paper. She has lived on a shoestring since she left her husband around 2001. She lives entirely off of her writing income so that she can be a stay-at-home single mother for her youngest child.

An internationally known author, her website, **annienygma.com** is one of the top minimalism/simplicity blogs on the Internet and she has written over 30 books on a variety of subjects. Though she officially retired at the age of 41, she doesn't plan to ever stop writing.

Even now Annie still insists on living cheap. She limits her monthly expenses to $500 a month or less by using the tips found in this book and others that she has written.

She currently resides in Central Kentucky with her daughter and a small menagerie of pets. Her days are spent writing books, working on her website, reading copiously and visiting with friends and family.

It is her desire to help others through the written word. If this book has benefited you in any way she asks that you help others by leaving an honest review on the website where you purchased your copy.

Connect With Annie Online

Annie loves to hear from her readers. If you have the chance, she asks that you send her an email or visit her online to say hello.

Website:
http://annienygma.com

Email:
http://annienygma.com/contact/

Twitter:
http://www.twitter.com/annienygma

Facebook:
http://www.facebook.com/annienygma

Smashwords:
http://www.smashwords.com/profile/view/annienygma

Do You Want to Live on Less?

Would you like to learn how from someone who actually does?

Over ten years ago I found myself a single mother with three children to raise.

I had to learn fast.

I had to support those kids on a fast food paycheck while I put myself through school.

Not only did I manage to do it but I topped my own expectations. We ended up living better than I ever would have imagined.

Since then I have not only quit my day job but I have built up sufficient income to become a single stay-at-home mother to my youngest child. This feat would not have been possible without the frugality of shoestring living.

We live well on about $500 a month - and know how to live on even LESS!

Over the years I have shared my secrets with others who have fallen on hard times. I have helped friends who became disabled, single parents, the unemployed and others who found a need to live on as little money as possible.

The first thing I always shared was the timeless words of my grandmother. Even now I can hear her reminding me to hold up my head because...

"There's no sin in being poor!"

This may be your first brush with life below the poverty line. You may be scared. You may be ashamed. You may not know what to do or where to start.

I'm here to help you save money

I have drawn upon my 10+ years of personal experience to create the ultimate frugal living guide. I won't bore you with stupid fluff about clipping coupons. Instead, you will find a concise method you can implement to save thousands of dollars over the course of a year.

Sections Include:

Housing
Auto
Groceries (Includes raising food)
Computers (includes where to find free and inexpensive software)
Television (includes watching shows online for free)
Books (lots of links to free ebooks and how to search for free ebooks online)
Music (includes links for free music sites)
Clothing
Cleaning tips and recipes
Personal care tips and recipes Furniture
Thrift Shops
Yard Sales
Jobs and self-employment
And much more!

I not only explain the exact methods that I use to save money and live frugally but I also explain how I could live on about half of the money that I actually do.

While you may not wish to apply everything here I am confident that you will be inspired to save more money than you ever thought possible. You will learn the skills you need to overcome your current financial challenge.

Start Saving Money Today!

Do You Have Any Tips?

Do you have any money saving tips that you would like to share? Send them to **http://annienygma.com/contact/** with "Tips" in the subject line and I will send you a FREE PDF copy of *"The Shoestring Girl"* that you can keep for yourself or share with a friend.

CONGRATULATIONS!

YOU HAVE REACHED THE END!

Thank you for your support!

Please leave an honest review of this book on the website where you purchased it to help others determine if this book will help them. Send a link for the published review to *http://annienygma.com/contact* with the words "PDF Request" in the subject line to receive a FREE PDF of this book to share with a friend. Thank you!

THE END

Notes:

Notes:

Notes:

Notes:

www.ingramcontent.com/pod-product-compliance
Lightning Source LLC
Chambersburg PA
CBHW071405170526
45165CB00001B/187